This journal belongs to:

....

Instagram

@limitlessabundance_official

info@limitlessabundanceofficial.com

@limitlessabundance

Sis, it's time to take care of yourself!

This is a letter of self-love and self-worth to you, our beautiful Black woman. We're writing this to tell you of the beautiful complexity of who you are and how important it is that you begin to embrace this complexity. Yes, you are powerful and capable of anything that you put your mind to, but don't let the rest of the world convince you that you are not soft, tender, and vulnerable too.

To quote Emmy Meli: *You are woman, you are fearless, you are sexy, you are divine, you are unbeatable, you are creative, and the rest of the world can get in line.* There is so much to you, dear Black woman, and that intricacy requires love, care, and dedication to thrive.

Many of us have become so fixated on tearing down the patriarchy and demolishing the adverse systems of sexism and racism that have been institutionalized in our societies. While these are highly remarkable and hugely significant goals, we shouldn't lose our self-love in the hatred that we have for these things.

We hate the history of unjustified suffering, pain, and hardship that these things have caused the Black woman for far too long. And while our anger is 100% justified, we cannot let righteous fury overpower the love that we should have for ourselves. The love that we should have for our identity. Our culture. Our heritage. Our families. Our communities.

So as you fight the good fight, always remember that love conquers all. As you tell the world that you deserve everything and more, make yourself feel that worthiness. Give yourself a hug and a kiss, and then get up to give yourself all those beautiful things that you want for you.

Become highly intentional with your self-care. Stay aware of your acts of self-care as you perform them. Make them a big deal, because self-care is a big deal. See everything, big or small, that you do for your own good as self-care. This will breed heightened self-love and increase your self-worth. "I'm taking this walk for the good of my mind and body, and this is me practicing self-care." Being intentional about and conscious of your self-care will deepen your perception of yourself as a self-care-worthy woman.

Next, wear your worth like a crown that shines bright for all to see. Showing that you know your worth and you love every single perfect inch of you from top to bottom in a world that tried to steal your diamonds and cover your spark will unleash a superpower within you. Wielding that mindset, you will become limitless in the things that you can do and the things you can achieve. You will become a lighthouse that no one can ignore.

Keep your mind, body, and soul clean. Prioritize your health in all aspects; your physical, mental, emotional, and spiritual health. This is part of becoming intentional with your self-care. So whenever you meditate, analyze the state of your health in all these aspects, and then go ahead to do what is necessary to get yourself to optimal health on the whole.

Now, here are 8 tips for Black women that will help you to achieve your goal of thriving in life!

Live passionately

It's important to value your relationships and be passionate about whatever you do. You should never put anything above yourself, but to live a good life, you must live with passion. Many black women burn themselves out because they are engaged in relationships and doing things that they have no passion for. But when you are self-aware, self-compassionate, and self-confident, you will know what ignites your passion and your spirit, and those are things you should chase.

Don't be scared to try

Countless Black women have a dire fear of rejection when it comes to opportunities and striving for the things they want. This stems from a long history of the world telling us "No". But today, the world has come to embrace diversity a lot more than in the past, and Black women are being sought after more than ever, especially in settings ranging from academia to corporate environments.

So if you have a dream or a goal, whether in your personal, professional, academic, romantic, spiritual, or whatever aspect of your life, don't be scared to go for what you want. There's a high chance that your attempt at success will eventually grant you that win that you want. And even if you don't succeed, don't stop. Try again.

Set goals

To be able to live passionately and endeavor towards accomplishment, you need to have clear-cut goals, dreams, and/or aspirations. Having an end goal in sight is what will allow it to come into being. It will help you to chase the right opportunities and refuse the wrong ones with conviction. It will also save you a lot of time when it comes to making decisions because you'll already be certain of what you want and what's best for you.

You can make setting goals a daily activity that you do before you start your days off. You can also take some time to plan and pen down these goals in a journal so that you can always go back and re-read them.

Accept mistakes

Understand that you will make mistakes at certain points, and some changes will not always come as fast as you'd like them to. But that's okay, and coming to terms with that will help you learn the lessons better, rather than waste precious time beating yourself up.

Embrace change

One inevitable thing is change. Keep this in mind always so that when both the good and the bad changes happen, you'll be ready to face them head-on.

Be intentional with your self-care

We've probably said this 4 million times, but we'll say it again.

BE. INTENTIONAL. ABOUT. YOUR. SELF-CARE.

Don't be careless or casual with it. Don't let other things crowd it out. Don't put it last. Don't forget about it or skip it. Take care of yourself as a must. Intentional self-care will open you up to healing and winning faster than you can imagine.

Hype yourself, sis!

This could be in form of self-appreciation, self-promotion, or surrounding yourself with people that hype you too. Black women have been humble for too long. It's about time we blow our own trumpets, toot our own horns, and let the world know how powerful, brilliant, and successful we are. However, don't get into competitions with anybody; it'll always be you against you because you're the best!

Failure isn't the end of the world

Failure is just as bound to happen as success. But that doesn't mean that the world comes crashing down any time you fail. It's important to learn from failure and get back up. It may not be easy, but that's why you're a Black woman. There's nothing that you set your mind to that you can't achieve.

Hence, as unpredictable as life can be, live it to the fullest regardless of whether you win or you lose. You can always pick yourself up (or seek a helping hand if you need one), dust yourself off, and get back in the saddle.

Finally, dear Black woman, stay true to who you are always and seek a healthy balance in all that you do.

We can't wait to watch you thrive! ♡

The importance of self-care in Black women's lives

Black women are strong women. We are the pillars of the planet and the salt and spice of the earth. We are lovers, fighters, caregivers, protectors, innovators, creators, activists, and revolutionists. We are wives, mothers, daughters, sisters, cousins, bosses, workers, teachers, learners, and leaders. We are fierce, we are powerful, and we never give up.

All the qualities above and more are true; we Black women are really amazing. But in truth, as a Black woman, you've probably been told all of this before. Or you've heard or read about the "strength" of a black woman at some time in your life. These qualities are all things that Black women of all ages today get told about themselves all the time. However, one thing we hardly hear is how we Black women are also vulnerable, gentle, and tender. Because in as much as we cornerstones and powerhouses, we are also soft and worthy of so much care that we hardly receive.

Our long-standing unfamiliarity with our delicate sides as a result of having to be "strong" all our lives has led to a regrettable neglect of the intentional care that we ought to have been giving our minds, souls, and bodies for a long time now. Don't get me wrong. Being strong is good; it's an asset, not a liability. But in a bid to stay strong, we should not be overlooking our well-being. Strong, tall forest trees only stay alive because Mother Nature gives them all that they need to survive. A strong Black woman will only be able to stay strong and beautiful when she puts her self-care needs first and ensures that she's given everything that she needs to thrive.

Why is self-care so important for Black women – especially now

The importance of self-care in Black women's lives can never be over-emphasized. We're now in a new year where everyone must be trying to regroup, re-strategize, and run things in 2022 differently than they did last year. Hence, it is particularly important now that you're making your new year's resolutions to make prioritizing self-care one of the top things on your list.

The truth about self-care is that it is holistic in nature. It involves paying attention to everything including your physical, mental, emotional, and spiritual well-being. Furthermore, self-care shouldn't be just a once-in-a-week kind of affair. It's something that you need to plan and incorporate into your daily life. Every day should be a self-care day - that's how important your self-care needs to be.

Now, you've heard that self-care is important more than a few times, but why exactly is it important, especially for a Black woman? Well, sis, there are a ton of reasons why self-care is very important for us as Black women and we'll be sharing them with you. Each reason is going to prove to you that now is the time to take care of yourself!

The struggles, challenges, and barriers we face as Black women

It's one thing to be a woman and have to deal with sexism in different facets of your life coming from both men and at times even women. It's another to be Black and face racism, colorism, and all other kinds of prejudice against your skin color. And it's an entirely different ballpark when you're a Black woman dealing with both sets of prejudices at the same time.

Then imagine being a Black woman who also falls under other minority groups. A Black woman who is also a member of the LGBTQ+ community or who falls under the low-income earning class. Having to also deal with homophobia and/or class oppression.

The life of a Black woman is hardly ever a walk in the park. It is oftentimes ridden with wars and struggles and obstacles. Because of her womanhood and the color of her skin, she has to struggle to get a chance at high-paying jobs, good education, adequate healthcare, a career in politics or even to climb up in any career at all, and a whole lot of other things that are easily handed to men and other women. Out of all 49 vice presidents that the United States has ever had, Kamala Harris is the first woman and the first African-American. It took over two centuries for a Black

American woman to get her chance.

Things may be better now than they were just a couple of decades back owing to the rise of numerous civil rights movements, but Black women shouldn't have to struggle at all. We deserve the same ease that is handed to others on a platter.

For a long, long time, the world has been cruel to Black lives and Black identities, most especially to us, the female portion of the Black race. We've been through years of slavery, racism, sexism, being told that who we were wasn't enough, that our skin was ugly, our hair unruly, our eyes too dark, our noses and lips too big, our bodies overweight, our manner of speech "ghetto", our entire beings undeserving of the same treatment that was given to others.

So beyond simply fighting for change, we also need to heal from history. We aren't always handed the same luxuries on platters that others get, and we may well never be. So we have to make it our responsibility to hand these things to ourselves. To give ourselves the healing and the compassion that we need. And radical self-care is the perfect place to start.

The ways we were raised

9 times out of 10, you will find that a Black woman was raised in a specific manner. She was taught right from her childhood years to be selfless, to repress her emotions, and always put others first. Furthermore, as we grew up, some of us may have even noticed a pattern in which we've found ourselves oftentimes being treated as more masculine than feminine. As if

our femininity is something that can easily be discounted from our identity as Black women.

We may have been taught to be selfless, but self-care isn't selfish. It isn't overindulgent. It is the care and self-prioritization that all Black women deserve.

You shouldn't be afraid to demand what you deserve. To defy societal expectations and put your needs, goals, and well-being above all else. To get radical with your self-care and put yourself first.

Self-care is what will liberate you from the chains of generations of historical and familial patterns of suppressed pain, trauma, and hardship - all in a bid to make ourselves smaller so that others can feel better about themselves. Self-care will help you to rediscover who you truly are and wholeheartedly embrace your own dignity, value, and self-worth.

Mental enslavement

Despite the many of us that are still clamoring for change, a lot of Black women have given up. Scores of Black women have surrendered themselves to the little that society has squeezed out to them. They have settled for the bare minimum that has been assigned as their worth because they are simply weary of the war.

This is known as mental enslavement. The ingrained belief that your struggles will always be bigger than you, so you stop trying to fight them at all even if you have the power to. What mental enslavement does is that it holds us back from realizing our full potentials. It makes us lose sight of our vision and settle for less than we are really worth.

Slowly, self-doubt, feelings of inferiority, the fear of trying, and unproductiveness creep in, and your mental enslavement can even lead to you letting others exploit you. The only way to break out of these things is to revive your self-love, self-worth, and self-appreciation.

This is where self-care comes in. Your first step towards liberating yourself and your mind might just be to begin letting go of any hurt or toxicity and start out on your self-care journey towards healing.

"

If you

prioritize yourself,

you are going to

save yourself.

Gabrielle Union

Reasons why Black women often have difficulty practicing Radical Self-care

Audre Lorde, the late civil and feminist rights activist and writer, declared the act of self-care for Black women to be a radical thing, a political thing.

So what is this "Radical Self-care" that Audre spoke of?

Radical self-care is simply prioritizing the responsibility that you have to take care of yourself first before considering what others need. Your needs come first before you begin to consider what others may require from you. It involves fully embracing practices that keep you physically and psychologically fit and healthy, and having no regrets when it comes to putting yourself first in any way.

Radical self-care is a Black woman's political statement: she's taking back every good thing that society has deprived her of and giving them to herself because that's what she deserves.

Unfortunately, many Black women often find it difficult to

practice radical self-care. The main reason for this is simply that we are usually prone to put everyone and everything first, leaving our self-care at the bottom of our to-do lists, or sometimes even excluded from the list entirely.

Other reasons include leading a genuinely busy life, allowing the things that you see and read on the internet to negatively affect your emotional space, the safety risk of outdoor self-care practices like taking a walk through your neighborhood, and the absence of a community to motivate you.

However, if a Black woman were to become seriously intentional about practicing radical self-care, there are so many ways to circumvent these obstacles.

If you find that you always come last in your plans, make the words "Me first" a mantra and say them to yourself all the time so that you always remember that you have to put yourself first. Too busy? Then plan out your schedule to squeeze in just the littlest, easiest bits of helpful self-care such as morning yoga, taking little breaks, and meditation.

Is social media getting too overwhelming and cutting at your self-image? Then limit your social media time and only follow accounts that encourage you to become a better you. Facing outdoor safety risks? Then take safety precautions; don't let apprehension get in the way of your self-care. Feeling unmotivated? There are so many online communities and forums for Black women where you can find like-minded self-care enthusiasts that will give you all the motivation you need.

The best thing about radical self-care is that it keeps you true to yourself. The things that matter to you will always be given priority, you'll be constantly challenged to keep growing, and it will become so much easier to find satisfaction in life. Radical self-care puts the steering wheel totally in your hands, and you gain the confidence to determine how much of yourself you give to others and even refuse others when it's the best thing for you.

Protect your magic, Sis.

We will always encourage every Black woman to practice self-care because it is so important for us. It is important now more than ever because, for way too long, we haven't been afforded the opportunities the same way other women have to practice radical self-care. And it's about time that changed for good

There's a new sheriff in town and her first order of duty: Black women will be prioritizing our self-care, all day, every day. We are going to be protecting our magic, doing everything for our benefits and our well-beings, and becoming our most energetic, most productive, most amazing selves!

A few things that we should note before diving into the tips. Self-care is easy. It's not something that has to be a huge extravaganza. You don't have to empty your savings on expensive vacations, luxury spa days, and top-dollar gifts in order to practice self-care (although if these are things that make you happy, by all means, get them all sis!). Self-care can really be so simple because there are so many little acts of self-care that you can incorporate into your daily routine.

Likewise, you need to remember that self-care is all-encompassing. Every aspect of you matters: your physical health, mental state, emotional well-being, and spiritual awareness. One cannot thrive when the other isn't. Thus, you will notice that a lot of the benefits that you get from various self-care practices span across all four of these aspects to show you how interconnected they are.

Now, let's get into the daily self-care tips that will soon make you a pro at putting yourself first. And while all of these tips are amazing, remember that you can take them all at your own pace. Implement them one at a time until you've carved out a self-care routine that you are 100% content and comfortable with.

Self-care tips for Black women

Daily affirmations

We Black women are worth so much, and then even much more than that. Affirming this every day is a good way to keep yourself cognizant of that fact so that nothing and no one can convince you otherwise. These affirmations can be positive statements about yourself that you can write down in your journal or a digital note, then read and reaffirm them daily. This practice will help you overcome negative and self-sabotaging thoughts. It's also a great way to manifest positive things into your life as well as your dreams into reality.

Part of these affirmations should be you appreciating yourself for all that you are and all that you do. Tell yourself that you are doing a great job when you have put in your best in your workplace, at home, in your relationships, wherever! The best kind of "Thank you" is the kind that you say to yourself in appreciation of the efforts that you make every day. Hearing words of gratitude from others may be nice, but the best appreciation comes from within.

After thanking yourself, express your gratitude for all the things that are going well for you and even the things that are not going so well but still form part of the experiences that you get to learn valuable lessons from. Doing all of this will cultivate a spirit of gratitude within you, which will help you to always see the bright side of life even on gloomy days. Trust that there will always be something to be grateful for; even simply waking up in the morning is a huge blessing.

Finally, look in the mirror every chance you get and tell the woman that you see there, "I love you." Day by day, strengthen your self-love and self-worth by doing loving self-care acts for yourself.

What's best for you is what works

We may be Black women as one group, but we are all tremendously unique in our own way. The stereotypes that have been placed on us by society may say otherwise, but we are all different and special. Therefore, what may work for the next person may not be the same routine that would work for you. This is why it is important to pay close attention to yourself and what your needs are precisely to determine what self-care practices will work best for you.

Self-care will always be all about you, so don't get side-tracked into focusing on everything that someone else may be doing. You can take some pointers but remain mindful of the fact that Janet's workouts or Aisha's skincare regimen are what works for them. You need to find what works best for you and stick to it. It may take some trial and error, but once you find the perfect self-care routine for you and then stay committed and intentional with it, you're going to fall in love with the results that you'll soon start to see.

Set your boundaries

Yes, it's super okay to say "No." Setting and enforcing your boundaries, be it at your job, in your relationships, or with people in general, will save you from a lot of unnecessary burdens and regrets. You should make it a priority to always politely refuse any requests to your time, energy, and resources that would make you go unnecessarily or unwantedly out of your way if you were to otherwise assent.

It only takes that two-letter word to preserve your sanity because no matter what you do, you can never please everyone. So you might as well start learning to tell people "No".

Physical care

There's this misconception that self-care just has to do with your mental health. But like we stated, self-care is all-inclusive. Your physical, mental, emotional, and spiritual health all go hand in hand. When it comes to caring for your physical fitness, we all know the basics. Exercising, body maintenance, and eating right. But do you the immense benefits that these things actually provide you with?

You know the physical benefits that come with working out, such as getting that "perfect" waist to hip ratio and having your clothes fit more flatteringly. But did you know that exercise also helps to improve your mood, reduce your stress levels, make your sleep better, and brighten your spirit?

That all those body care regimens—from caring for your hair to your skin, teeth, hands, and feet—all help to boost your confidence, make you feel more relaxed, protect you from sickness, and give you a more positive mindset?

That a healthy diet not just improves your gut health and helps you maintain a moderate weight, but it also improves your memory and brain health, prevents depression and fatigue, reduces the risk of cancer, and influences you to make other healthy lifestyle choices?

Again, your physical, mental, emotional, and spiritual health always go hand in hand. So whatever you're doing for the good of your body will also have wonderful impacts on your soul, emotions, and mind as well. Therefore, this is a sign that you should start taking serious care of your body today.

Drink water

Every Black woman we know says, "Drink water and mind your business", but are y'all really doing that? It's such a simple act that goes a very long way but many of us aren't practicing what we preach. Water is a substance that detoxes your body both physically and spiritually. It cleanses, heals, makes you feel better, and gives you more mental clarity and energy. This is why it is so important to drink a sufficient amount of water daily.

For a woman, it is medically advised that you drink approximately 3 liters of fluids daily—fluids meaning water, other beverages, and fluids in food.

Make Happiness a Habit

This is another great self-care habit to add to your list. When you're up to your eyeballs in all the things that you have to get done daily, it's so easy to forget to make space for things that make you happy. You need to make a conscious effort to laugh heartily every day; life's too short not to see the humor that exists everywhere. Listen to some good music. Sing. Dance. Do a spin. Forget whoever's watching and make yourself happy whenever you get the chance, because joy is a blissful way to renew your spirit.

Meditate

Living a fast-paced, busy life can get to be too much very quickly. And so it's important to take time out to slow down and put your thoughts, actions, and decisions into perspective. Meditation gives you the best avenue to do this. It also helps you to keep your mental space clear and organized, which, in turn, will manifest physically into attracting good things and good people to you.

Time to slow down and reflect is also the best time to recite your affirmations. Another tip is to meditate in the early hours of the morning, just after you've woken up. This will help you to ease into your day at a more peaceful and composed pace, rather than jumping out of bed up and diving headfirst into a disorderly rush.

Toss out the toxicity

When it comes to protecting your magic and your energy, all sources of negativity need to be tossed out of the window. And don't hesitate to toss. Toss all day if you need to. You're putting yourself first, sis, so if something is bad for you in any way, then it needs to go now. And this could be anything from your work, to a person, or even a habit you may have. Toss out that toxicity and believe me, it's going to be one of the things you'll tell yourself "Thank you" for in the near future.

Be open to seeking help

Don't shy away from asking for help when you need it. I know many Black women like to believe that they're strong enough not to need any outright assistance, but it's okay to not be strong sometimes. It's okay to need help. It could be from a mental health professional or from your parent, spouse, or a trusted friend.

Sometimes, having support is the only way we can get through certain things, so when you need help, please ask for it.

Self-therapy tip: Journaling

Therapeutic journaling is another way to obtain new perspectives of yourself and your experiences by making you take a deep dive into your inner space and take an extensive look at your pre-existing perceptions of things. When you keep a journal, you write down your thoughts, emotions, and experiences, and this can be very cathartic for a Black woman.

Self-care is especially important during these stressful times to ensure that we protect our well-being and happiness. Therefore, we Black women must allow ourselves to be open and honest about what we need from ourselves and those around us. We should be bold and unapologetic in our radical self-care habits because...

we are worthy of it.

PART I
EMOTIONAL
Self-Care

"

You wanna fly,

you got to give up the sh*t that
weighs you down.

Toni Morrison

Emotional self-care

Emotional self-care is caring for your emotional needs by identifying what it is you're feeling and then moving forward in a way that honors yourself and those emotions. It may include activities that help you acknowledge and express your feelings regularly and safely.

How to practice emotional self-care

✦ *Show yourself that you can exhibit any range of emotion freely and openly.*

✦ *Allow yourself to feel. Do not try to suppress any negative feelings such as anger, fear, or frustrations.* The most important step to emotional self care is allowing yourself to feel and experience the emotions that come to you. Try as much as possible to express them and move on to the next positive thing. Take a few deep breaths, especially before expressing your feelings. Honor and respect your feelings and emotions, experience them without judgment, guilt, or embarrassment. You can always choose to let them go.

✦ *Say yes to yourself and your needs.* Put your own needs first. Stop over-explaining yourself to others. Many of us really struggle with putting ourselves first. When you take care of yourself, you create a better place for yourself to live in. Switching your focus to yourself is the best thing you can do, not only for yourself but for others.

+ *Don't be too hard on yourself and the people around you.* You are all trying your best and it's only a matter of time before your hard work pays off. Allow yourself to make mistakes. Try again when moments don't go as planned.

+ *Concentrate on the things that are within your control.* While we cannot choose what happens to us, we do get to choose how we respond to those circumstances.

+ *Protect your energy from others.* Surround yourself with people who lift you up and make you feel good.

+ *Identify triggers to your emotions.*

+ *Create boundaries.* Learn to say no. Boundaries are essential when it comes to emotional self care, they are necessary for your wellbeing.

+ *Practice self-compassion daily.* Take time out to reflect.

+ If you find that the stuff on social media is driving you nuts, you should take a break. While information is good, you don't want to sacrifice your emotional well-being for it.

+ *Become aware of your inner critic and your limiting beliefs.*

+ *Make a habit of expressing gratitude for the blessing in your life.* Everyone has at least one thing to be thankful for.

+ *Ask for help when necessary.* Call on others for help when you start to feel overwhelmed.

+ *Schedule time to rest, do something you love each day, have some fun and enjoy life!*

Journey to self-love & self-discovery

What does self-love mean to me?

....

....

....

Things I love about myself...

....

....

....

I can be my authentic self when...

....

....

....

In what ways do I show love for myself?

....

....

....

What is something I have always wanted to try but never have?

....

What am I holding onto that isn't serving me anymore?

....

....

....

When was the last time I felt beautiful, smart, or fearless?

....

....

....

How often do I spend time and energy taking care of myself
versus taking care of others?

....

....

....

When was the last time I told myself *"good job, I'm proud of you"*?

....

....

How often do I take on other people's problems as if they were
my own?

....

....

....

Do I believe I'm worthy of good things like love and happiness?

....

....

....

What do I need to be more at peace with myself?

....

....

....

Do I speak up when I feel I'm not getting what I deserve?

....

....

....

Do I feel guilty if I put my needs first?

....

....

....

How comfortable am I with saying *"no"* to things or people who don't bring me joy?

....

....

....

....

How important is my own happiness?

....

....

....

How often do I apologize, even when it's not my fault?

....

....

....

Do I give myself the same care and kindness I give to others?

....

....

....

How content am I with my life in general?

....

....

....

....

....

....

....

....

A vow to myself

I..,

vow to love myself, to love all of my flaws, and to put myself and my best interest first.

I vow to let myself feel my emotions.

I deserve the world and even a little more.

I will live the life that I want and deserve.

Today and for the rest of my days, I choose to love myself, cherish myself, and to accept myself, just the way that I am.

....
MY SIGNATURE

Self-improvement

What aspects of your life do you want to improve and why?

....

....

....

....

....

What steps would you need to start taking to manifest these improvements?

....

....

....

....

....

How will your life look like after the improvements? What happens if you do not follow through with the changes in a year?

....

....

....

....

Self assessment

This assessment is concerned with your own thoughts, opinions and feelings. At the end of this assessment is a little box where you can note down the aspects you'd like to improve upon and how you plan to do it.

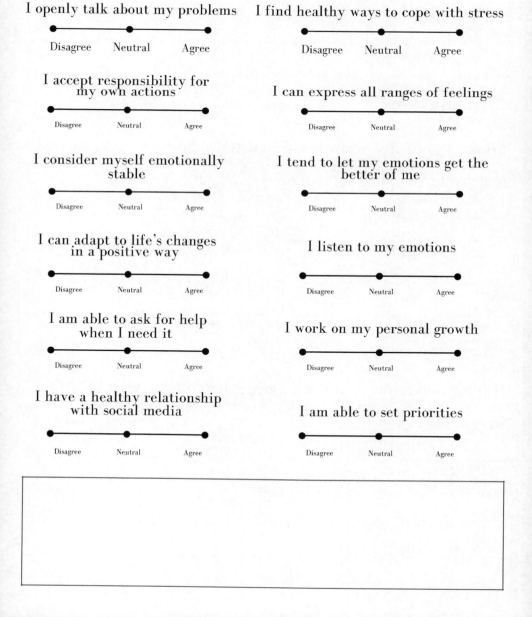

I openly talk about my problems

Disagree   Neutral   Agree

I find healthy ways to cope with stress

Disagree   Neutral   Agree

I accept responsibility for my own actions

Disagree   Neutral   Agree

I can express all ranges of feelings

Disagree   Neutral   Agree

I consider myself emotionally stable

Disagree   Neutral   Agree

I tend to let my emotions get the better of me

Disagree   Neutral   Agree

I can adapt to life's changes in a positive way

Disagree   Neutral   Agree

I listen to my emotions

Disagree   Neutral   Agree

I am able to ask for help when I need it

Disagree   Neutral   Agree

I work on my personal growth

Disagree   Neutral   Agree

I have a healthy relationship with social media

Disagree   Neutral   Agree

I am able to set priorities

Disagree   Neutral   Agree

My achievements

What are the things you feel most proud of? Name at least three

....

....

....

....

....

Looking at the list above, explain why do these things make you feel proud?Are they something you've made an effort to achieve?

....

....

....

....

....

If you could achieve only one more great thing in your life, what would it be?

....

....

....

....

Values

What are the things you value in life? What are your priorities?

....

....

....

List the three most important things for you. Things that give your life meaning.

....

....

....

How much time are you spending on the things you value the most?

....

....

....

If you're not spending enough time on your highest priority items then what steps can you take to change that?

....

....

....

Perceptions

How is your public persona different compared to your private persona? In your own opinion, what are the reasons for the differences?

....

....

....

What do you want people to know you for? What do you want them to say when talking about you?

....

....

....

Who are the people you feel most comfortable with? Who are the people you feel like you can be your true self?

....

....

....

What places and activities make you feel alive and truly yourself?

....

....

The obituary exercise

If I died tomorrow, would I die happy?

....

....

....

....

....

Am I happy with the direction my life is going? What could I improve? What am I missing from my life?

....

....

....

....

....

What would I like to be remembered for? What steps can I take right now to start making that happen?

....

....

....

....

My patterns

What are some things that you feel keep constantly happening in your life?

....

....

....

....

....

Why do you think these things keep happening? What have you learned from them?

....

....

....

....

....

What steps could you take right now to start breaking a bad patterns and/or enforcing a new and more positive pattern?

....

....

....

Relationships

People I am grateful for in my life...

....

....

Why I am grateful to have them...

....

....

People I admire...

....

....

Why I admire them...

....

....

People I can always rely on...

....

....

People that always support more...

....

....

Boundaries

What are the biggest things that stop you from setting and holding boundaries?

....

....

....

....

I struggle setting boundaries with these people...

....

....

....

....

I struggle setting boundaries with them because...

....

....

....

I feel most angry and frustrated when they...

....

....

....

Boundaries

Write down the unhealthy boundaries in your relationships. Mention the ways in which you can replace them with healthy boundaries.

Unhealthy boundaries in my relationships	Ways to improve them and replace them with healthy ones
e.g. No recognition of my emotions / controlling behavior	*e.g. Knowing that my needs and feelings are just as important as the needs and feelings of others.*

Anxiety

What situations trigger your anxiety?

....

....

....

....

Do you worry about lots of different things?

....

....

....

....

Do you have trouble controlling your worries?

....

....

....

I feel most comfortable when...

....

....

....

....

Managing anxiety

What is stressing me out?

....

....

....

....

What can I do about it?

....

....

....

....

Good ways to distract myself ...

....

....

....

People I can ask for advice...

....

....

....

....

Anxiety & Triggers

Date and Time	Trigger What was happening before I began to feel anxious?	Symptoms Physical Emotional Behavioral	Outcome What helped me to calm down?	Anxiety Rating How intense was my anxiety? (1 - low ; 10 - high)

Mindfulness exercise

Do I tend to obsess about the past or worry about the future?

....

....

....

....

....

....

Does either obsessing about he past or worrying about the future help me deal with the present?

....

....

....

....

What are ways I can do to stay grounded and be present?

....

....

....

....

,,

When you take care of yourself,

you're a better person

for others.

Solange Knowles

S.T.O.P.
technique

S   *Stop.* In this first step, we will allow ourselves to take a moment to recognize that there are strong emotions involved in this situation or that we simply need to have a moment for ourselves.

T   *Take a Breath.* Breathe, Next, we will calm our nerves by taking a breath and drawing our attention back to our body Take as much, or as little time as you need here.

O   *Observe.* Think about what you're feeling right now. Start with your body is your heart rate elevated? Sweaty palms"), then move to your emotions (Which emotions do you feel specifically?), and finally examine your thoughts (What thoughts come from and are influencing your beliefs?). This will help to reveal your true beliefs and insights.

P   *Proceed with Wisdom.* As you reach the end of the practice, consider the personal insights you've come to realize. Use these to determine what a wise course of action would be in order to get into a more positive mindset and proceed effectively.

5 4 3 2 1
Coping technique

5 Acknowledge 5 things you see around you. It could be a pen, a spot on the ceiling, anything in your surroundings

4 Acknowledge 4 things you can touch around you. It could be your hair, a pillow, or the ground under your feet.

3 Acknowledge 3 things you hear. This could be any external sound. If you can hear your belly rumbling that counts! Focus on things you can hear outside of your body.

2 Acknowledge 2 things you can smell. Maybe you are in your office and smell pencil, or maybe you are in your bedroom and smell a pillow. If you need to take a brief walk to find a scent you could smell soap in your bathroom, or nature outside.

1 Acknowledge 1 thing you can taste. What does the inside of your mouth taste like - gum, coffee, or the sandwich from lunch?

Forgiveness

I forgive myself for...	Next time I will...

Vision board

Write down key points in each category describing what your ideal life would look like. This worksheets is designed to give you an idea of things you would want to strive for. You may think that you don't need to write it down, but writing it down makes it more real and creates a commitment that compels you to move forward to achieve your dreams and goals. Try to write in present tense.

Personal Growth

....

....

....

....

Health & Wellness

....

....

....

....

Family

....

....

....

....

Love & Relationships

....

....

....

....

Career

....

....

....

....

Finances

....

....

....

....

Home Life

....

....

....

....

....

Thoughts

In the clouds, write words to describe your thoughts and feelings.

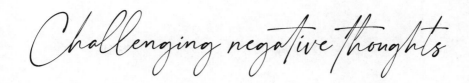

Challenging negative thoughts

What is the most troubling thought that is troubling me?

....

....

....

What evidence suggests that this thought is true? What evidence suggests that this thought is false?

....

....

....

....

Am I jumping to conclusions? To feel better I need to keep in mind...

....

....

What do I think of the original thought now? (Sum up your new way of thinking)

....

....

....

Reframe your thoughts

Negative thoughts	Positive thoughts
e.g. I don't deserve a good life.	*e.g. I deserve to be happy and healthy.*

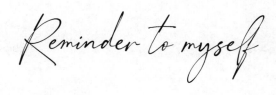

Reminder to myself

I like the fact that I...

....

....

....

....

My skills and strengths are...

....

....

....

....

I love being myself when...

....

....

....

The best event in my life was when...

....

....

....

....

PART II
SPIRITUAL
Self-Care

"

Every great dream begins with a

dreamer,

always remember, you have within
you the strength, the patience, and
the passion

to reach for the stars,

to change the world.

Harriet Tubman

Spiritual self-care

Spiritual self-care refers to any activities that nurtures your spirit and allows you to think bigger than yourself. Spiritual self-care quiets the mind. Taking time for spiritual self-care is soul-fulfilling. Spiritual self-care is a ritual or practice that we do to further our connection with our higher self. Your higher self is who you truly are as an individual, the real you, your real self that is not overwhelmed or influenced by fear or ego. Spiritual self care does not have to be religious, although for some it is. Spirituality is a personal practice.

Aside from helping you build a stronger connection with your higher self, spiritual self-care has some other powerful benefits. For instance, if you seek inner peace, you should devote more time to practicing spiritual self-care.

How to practice spiritual self-care

✦ *Meditate regularly.* Meditation allows us to slow down. Meditation is a powerful practice that can bring you closer to your higher self and can give you a clearer connection to who you are and what you want out of life.

✦ *Use positive affirmations.* They can be your way to speak to your higher power.

✦ *Practice gratitude.* Practicing gratitude is spiritual in nature.

✦ *Spend time in nature.* Being in nature heals. In nature, you are truly in the moment Nature can be very healing because it allows us to experience a moment with all five senses.

✦ *Find a spiritual community to connect with.*

✦ *Get a mentor or a spiritual advisor.*

✦ *Clear your space.* To ensure your soul is cared for you need to ensure that your environment is at the optimal vibrational level. Removing bad energy from your space is a powerful spiritual self-care practice. Let in positive energy.

✦ *Journal.*

✦ *Read inspiring, uplifting, spiritual books.* They can make a huge difference on your outlook on life.

✦ *Practice yoga.* Yoga is a journey into the soul.

✦ *Unplug from technology.* Use it responsibly, avoid checking your phone all the time.

✦ *Align with the moon's cycle.*

✦ *Experiment with tarot cards, crystals, and other spiritual tools.*

My spirituality

Has my outlook on religion and/or spirituality changed over the years? If so, how?

....
....
....

How important is spirituality to my life now?

....
....
....

How deeply am I connected with my soul?

....
....
....

What experiences have most shaped my spiritual life?

....
....
....
....

What does the term 'spiritual growth' mean to me?

....

....

....

....

....

What signs or synchronicities has the universe sent me
recently?

....

....

....

....

....

What am I most grateful for in this moment?

....

....

....

....

....

What lesson has spirit taught me recently?

....

....

Write about a moment when you felt most spiritually alive and connected to the divine.

....
....
....
....
....
....
....
....
....

What are my darker shadow traits?

....
....
....
....
....
....
....
....
....

How often do I follow my intuition?

....

....

....

....

....

How can I connect more deeply with the natural world around me?

....

....

....

....

....

Do I enjoy spending time alone?

....

....

....

....

How am I connected to the divine and the universe?

....

....

....

Self assessment

Spirituality can be defined generally as an individual's search for ultimate or sacred meaning and purpose in life. At the end of this assessment is a little box where you can note down the aspects you'd like to improve upon and how you plan to do it.

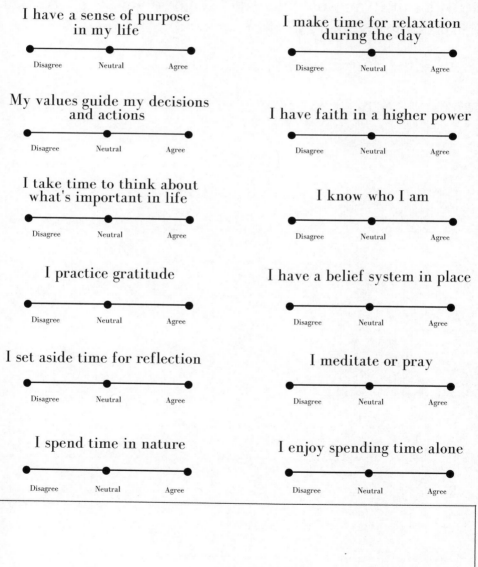

I have a sense of purpose in my life

Disagree · Neutral · Agree

I make time for relaxation during the day

Disagree · Neutral · Agree

My values guide my decisions and actions

Disagree · Neutral · Agree

I have faith in a higher power

Disagree · Neutral · Agree

I take time to think about what's important in life

Disagree · Neutral · Agree

I know who I am

Disagree · Neutral · Agree

I practice gratitude

Disagree · Neutral · Agree

I have a belief system in place

Disagree · Neutral · Agree

I set aside time for reflection

Disagree · Neutral · Agree

I meditate or pray

Disagree · Neutral · Agree

I spend time in nature

Disagree · Neutral · Agree

I enjoy spending time alone

Disagree · Neutral · Agree

Brainstorm self-care activities

Self-care activities are those things we do to take care of our spiritual, mental, emotional, and physical health. Create a list of as many potential self-care activities as possible. Only include activities that you would genuinely enjoy doing. (e.g. try yoga, balanced diet, regular exercise)

....

....

....

....

....

....

....

....

....

....

....

....

....

....

....

....

Self-care vision board

Create a self-care vision board. A self-care vision board is a collection of images and words that reflect your ideas for self-care. Putting your dreams and goals on paper can help you to manifest your desire. When you feel lost or unsure about your manifesting process, or even get frustrated, check back on your goals and insights to find guidance.

You can either work on multiple changes or one change at a time. Being intentional about your goals will aid in making them feel more possible. Start searching for things like self-love quotes, positive images that correspond with your chosen self-care activities, self care tips, and anything else you would want to add to your self-care vision board.

Be bold and creative.

All of this serves to motivate you to work on your self-care practice. Everything happening in your life is a reflection of what is happening inside of you. Your world is a reflection of you. Whatever you focus on will take shape and manifest into your daily life. It's so important to know exactly how to use your manifesting power.

Self-care vision board

Self-care vision board

Self-care positive affirmations

- ✦ *Regardless of my circumstances, I have the power to thrive.*

- ✦ *I feed my body clean, nurturing food because I'm worth it.*

- ✦ *I am strong, empowered and capable of anything.*

- ✦ *I have the power to make the right choices for me.*

- ✦ *I care about myself and listen to all of my needs.*

- ✦ *I choose to learn more about my authentic self.*

- ✦ *I am deserving of all the good things in my life.*

- ✦ *I will turn negative thoughts into positive ones.*

- ✦ *My commitment to my self-care isn't selfish.*

- ✦ *I cherish the time I take to refill.*

- ✦ *I treat myself with compassion.*

- ✦ *I am in control of my thoughts.*

- ✦ *I am on the right path for me.*

- ✦ *I give myself room to grow.*

- ✦ *I am relaxed and at peace.*

- ✦ *I love and accept myself.*

Self-care positive affirmations

- ✦ I take care of the world when I take care of myself.

- ✦ I prioritize and practice self-care on the daily basis.

- ✦ I am choosing to focus on my self-care.

- ✦ I am regularly taking care of myself.

- ✦ I am patient and kind with myself.

- ✦ I take extra time to heal if I need it.

- ✦ I am in the process of healing.

- ✦ I am free from negative vibes.

- ✦ My life is filled with miracles.

- ✦ I am guided and protected.

- ✦ I am relaxed and at peace.

- ✦ I set healthy boundaries.

- ✦ I honor my intuition.

- ✦ I live with intention.

- ✦ I am a divine being.

- ✦ I am mentally well.

My affirmations

In this part you'll write down positive affirmations that will have a positive impact on the aspects of your life you're trying to improve.

A few important points:

First, always write your affirmations in present tense using "I" pronoun.

Second, use affirmative & positive words (avoid can't, won't, will not etc). For example "I'm full on energy and always take action", instead of "I'm not lazy".

Third, it's important to build a habit of using these affirmations when you're doing the opposite of what you know you should be doing.

"I'm not my mistakes", "I am worthy of good things", "Although I'm always striving for better, I'm good enough already", "Each day I strive to be a better person than I was yesterday".

RELATIONSHIPS

e.g. "I'm in control of the people I let in my life"

FINANCES

e.g. "I'm capable of creating my dream financial life"

CAREER

e.g. "I'm always striving to develop myself professionally"

HEALTH

e.g. "I'm in control of my physical fitness"

LOVE

e.g. "I have people who love me"

Gratitude

Gratitude is incredibly powerful. The best way to reach contentment is to want and feel grateful for what you already have. The magic words 'thank you' can give you everything that you want and more. As they say, it's better to lose count while naming your blessings than to lose your blessings to counting your troubles. Say 'thank you' everywhere you go and mean it. There is always a reason to be grateful and your gratitude should not depend on whether or not you already have what you want.

You are like a magnet that attracts or repels and so it is within your power to manifest the life that you truly deserve. Fill your life with light and love, in return, you will receive abundance and prosperity.

Gratitude journaling is one of the most powerful manifestation exercises. The benefits and the effects are almost endless and can be felt in nearly all areas of your life. Taking the time to write down everything you are grateful for can improve your self-esteem, help you feel relaxed and sleep better, help you stay positive, make you happier, reduce stress, and help keep your vibrational frequency on a high.

Gratitude journaling is a very simple practice that takes some time and commitment.

Gratitude

List 3 things you have a reason to be thankful for:

....

....

....

How are my challenges making me learn:

....

....

....

The people in my life I'm really thankful for:

....

....

....

Things I'm looking forward to:

....

....

....

....

....

....

Gratitude jar

Take some time to reflect on the people, experiences and the things you have in your life that you're really grateful for and put them in this gratitude jar! The goal is to fill up the jar up to the lid, so you can come back and reflect on things you've written down when you're feeling a bit down.

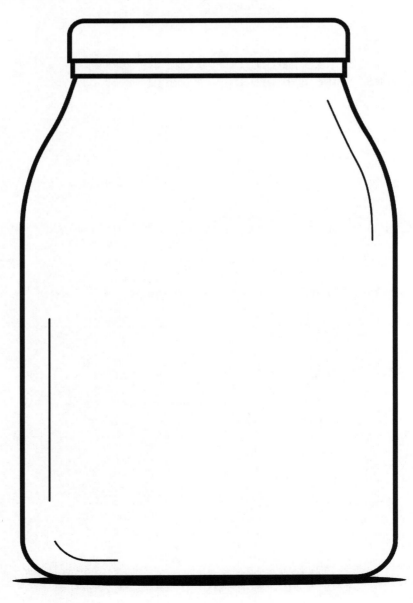

The small Things

I am grateful for things I can hear...

....

....

I am grateful for things I can taste...

....

....

I am grateful for things I can touch/feel...

....

....

I am grateful for things I can smell...

....

....

I am grateful for being able to...

....

....

I am grateful for these little things in my life...

....

....

Acts of kindness

Acts of kindness I have received...

....
....
....
....
....

Acts of kindness I have witnessed...

....
....
....
....
....

Acts of kindness I have done...

....
....
....
....
....
....

Experiences

Experiences I have had in my life that I'm grateful for...

....

....

....

....

....

....

....

....

What have I learned from these experiences?

....

....

....

....

....

....

....

....

Hopes and dreams

What are the things you like doing the most?

....

....

....

What are the things you would really like to do in your life?

....

....

....

What would you do if you had unlimited amount of money and never had to work again?

....

....

....

What would you do if you could not fail?

....

....

....

....

Who are some people who are living the life of your dreams?
What actions have these people taken to achieve such a life?

....
....
....
....
....
....

What steps and actions you can start taking right now to move
towards the life you described in the previous questions?

....
....
....
....
....

What will happen in one/five/ten years if you do not take these
actions? What will your life look like instead?

....
....
....
....
....

My dream life

In order to get to your goals that you want to achieve, we can work backwards by first describing your ideal life. What would your days consist of? What would you do in the mornings, evenings and nights? Where would you be and who would you be with? Remember, this is just an exercise to give you a vision to work towards - it's not set in stone and can change as you go along.

....

....

....

....

....

....

....

....

....

....

....

....

....

....

....

....

....

....

Limiting beliefs

Limiting belief	Source of the limiting belief	Examples where your belief was not true

Limiting beliefs

Limiting belief	Positive affirmation
e.g. I'll never be successful and free.	*e.g. I am smart and successful. I am worthy of financial security.*

"

You are where you are in life
because of what you

believe

is possible for yourself.

Oprah Winfrey

My bucket list

ACHIEVEMENTS	EXPERIENCES
On this side, write down all the things you want to ACHIEVE in your life - physically, financially, relationship wise, in your career etc.	On this side, write down all the things you want to EXPERIENCE in your life - happiness, new places, foods etc.

List of attractions

THINGS YOU HAVE ATTRACTED INTO YOUR LIFE	THINGS YOU WISH TO ATTRACT INTO YOUR LIFE

My inspiration

What are the things, places, experiences or people that get you motivated or excited in life? Are there any common themes among them?

....

....

....

....

....

....

....

....

What steps can you take and changes can you make to manifest more of these things, experiences and people in your life?

....

....

....

....

....

....

....

"

Don't underestimate yourself.

You are more capable than you think.

Misty Copeland

Manifestation worksheet

What I want to manifest...

....

....

....

....

How do I feel when I think about my desired reality?

....

....

....

....

How my life looks like when it finally arrives?

....

....

....

....

....

....

....

....

Manifestation worksheet

What I want to manifest...

....

....

....

....

How do I feel when I think about my desired reality?

....

....

....

....

How my life looks like when it finally arrives?

....

....

....

....

....

....

....

PART III
PHYSICAL
Self-Care

"

I need to see my own beauty and to continue to be reminded that

I am enough,

that I am worthy of love without effort, that I am beautiful, that the texture of my hair and that the shape of my curves, the size of my lips, the color of my skin, and the feelings that I have are all worthy and okay.

Tracee Ellis Ross

Physical self-care

Physical self care involves activities that improve your physical health such as diet and exercise. Physical self-care can also look like having a skincare routine, taking a hot bath, and getting outside in nature.

Health is a hot topic in the black community. Taking care of ourselves is of the utmost importance and so we need to ensure that we're not only eating the right food and exercising but that we also detox our minds. Think healthy thoughts and receive vitality in return.

We can heal hereditary conditions and avoid illnesses and diseases that are prevalent in the black community. It all starts with us being aware of what we entertain as truth and that we are in total control of our bodies. This physical vessel that our spirits are stored in response to the energy that we emit. We must make sure that we are in a high vibrational state whenever we can.

Through spiritual practices, we can gain better mental health, improve our perspective on how the body responds to vibrational frequencies and learn to heal from within. Though there is a place for modern medicine, we are powerful in ways that can change our entire anatomy. This is something that our ancestors practiced and that we should be aware of too. We need to achieve balance with the body, mind, and soul. Doing this can help us to attract more blessings into our lives and manifest miracles! This is something that all black women should keep in mind when we turn to spirituality.

How to practice physical self-care

+ *Exercise regularly.* Exercise releases natural endorphins, dopamine, serotonin, and adrenaline in your brain that help make you feel good. Start small and set achievable goals. For instance, you can start with 20 minutes a day, 3-5 times a week, and work your way up gradually.

+ *Sleep well and get enough rest.* Develop a regular sleep routine. Getting as much rest and sleep as possible is an essential physical self-care practice. Lack of sleep can have significant effect on your body and mind. According to experts, adults are expected to get at least 7-8 hours of sleep every day.

+ *Healthy diet.* Nourish yourself well. A healthy diet should contain lean proteins, fruits, and vegetables. Limit the intake of alcohol and caffeine. If you can, avoid processed foods. Spend some time and cook healthy, tasty and varied dishes.

+ *Stay hydrated.* While it may seem like a trivial act, drinking an adequate amount of water throughout the day can help your mind and body function at their best. Do not wait to feel thirsty, try to always have water nearby during all day.

Self assessment

A physical assessment can be helpful because it can help determine the status of your health. At the end of this assessment is a little box where you can note down the aspects you'd like to improve upon and how you plan to do it.

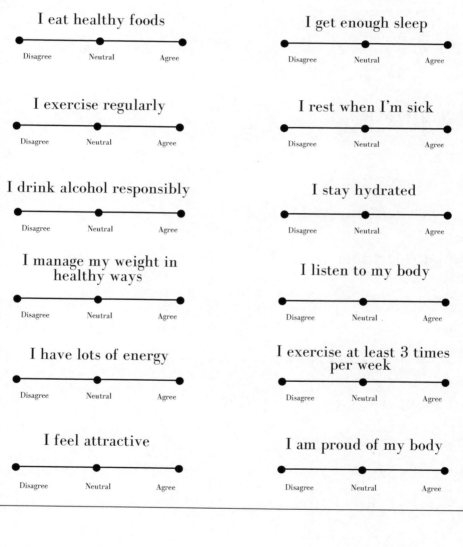

I eat healthy foods
Disagree   Neutral   Agree

I get enough sleep
Disagree   Neutral   Agree

I exercise regularly
Disagree   Neutral   Agree

I rest when I'm sick
Disagree   Neutral   Agree

I drink alcohol responsibly
Disagree   Neutral   Agree

I stay hydrated
Disagree   Neutral   Agree

I manage my weight in healthy ways
Disagree   Neutral   Agree

I listen to my body
Disagree   Neutral   Agree

I have lots of energy
Disagree   Neutral   Agree

I exercise at least 3 times per week
Disagree   Neutral   Agree

I feel attractive
Disagree   Neutral   Agree

I am proud of my body
Disagree   Neutral   Agree

Wellness questions

Ask yourself these questions to make healthy habits last.

Am I routinely investing in my health?

....

....

....

Do I eat healthy?

....

....

....

How do I feel after my meals?

....

....

....

Are my habits sabotaging my health?

....

....

....

....

....

Is it hard for me to relax?

....
....
....

Do I exercise? What are my favorite ways to move my body?

....
....
....

Does my day-to-day align with my larger values and long-term goals?

....
....
....
....
....

What is one thing I can do today to help me achieve my long-term goals?

....
....
....
....
....

What do I need to feel nourished, energized and strong?

....

....

....

What can I eliminate from my life that doesn't make me feel good?

....

....

....

Do I have the resources, tools, and support I need?

....

....

....

....

....

....

....

How can I make my home a self-care sanctuary?

....

....

....

....

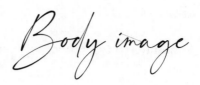

Body image

Ask yourself these questions to build a more positive body image.

If my body could talk right now, what would it say?

....

....

....

What beliefs and judgments do I have about myself and my body?

....

....

....

What helps me to feel comfortable in my own skin?

....

....

....

Is my appearance really important in how I evaluate my self-worth?

....

....

....

....

What does my body allow me to do?

....

....

....

....

....

How does my body help me do what I love?

....

....

....

What's one way I can celebrate my body every day?

....

....

....

What's something that makes me feel worse about my body?
(e.g. a scale at home, Instagram etc.)

....

....

Do I spend a lot of time worrying about what other people think
about my appearance?

....

....

Do I spend more time thinking about what I dislike about my appearance, than what I like about it?

....

....

....

....

Do my feelings about my appearance get in the way of accepting myself or enjoying my life?

....

....

....

What does a positive body image mean to me?

....

....

....

....

How are you, really?

....

....

....

....

....

Positive affirmation for body positivity

- My body is a gift. I treat it with love and respect.

- I am a brown skin beauty who knows her worth.

- I take care of my body because I matter.

- I define my worth and I am worthy.

- I tune in to what my body needs.

- I am confident in my body.

- I am worthy, whole and complete.

- I love my body as it is today.

- I celebrate my body's changes.

- My body deserves love and respect.

- I am comfortable in my own skin.

- My size does not determine my worth.

- My needs are just as important as anyone else's.

- I enjoy feeling good. It's okay for me to feel good.

- I am grateful for what my body is capable of doing.

- I am empowered to heal my body as best I can.

Create your own positive affirmations

I love my body and all of its uniqueness
I release all guilt and shame about my body

Habits

A habit is a pattern of behavior that is repeated on a regular basis. This behavior might take the form of action, a routine, or a way of life. What you do again and again shapes who you are.

Today, your life is simply the sum of your behaviors. As a result of your behaviors, how fit or out of shape are you? As a result of your behaviors, how successful or unsuccessful are you?

To choose which habit adjustments to undertake, first do an audit of your everyday activities. Take note of how you spend your time, energy, and attention. The most effective strategy to modify undesirable behaviors is to replace them with new ones.

Begin with tiny, simple modifications that you can implement on a daily basis. Celebrate every time you succeed in your habit! Feeling happy aids your brain's ability to wire in new actions, making them more likely to be repeated automatically.

Habit awareness

What negative habits are holding you back the most? What steps can you take to overcoming them?

....

....

....

....

....

....

....

What positive habits would you like to instill in yourself?

....

....

....

....

....

....

....

....

....

....

....

Build positive habits

Habits to break	Your ideal habits	What will your future self tell you if you don't start with this now?

Action brainstorm

Stop doing	
Do less	
Keep doing	
Do More	
Start doing	

"

I have a lot of things to prove to myself.

One is that I can live my life

fearlessly.

Oprah Winfrey

It's okay to...

It's okay to...
do what's best for me
to be myself

It's okay to...

It's okay to...

It's okay to...

It's okay to...

It's okay to...

Lifestyle goals for healthy living

Having goals is like having a map. You know where you are heading.

My goal	Most important steps to make it happen
	1. 2. 3. 4. 5.
	1. 2. 3. 4. 5.
	1. 2. 3. 4. 5.
	1. 2. 3. 4. 5.
	1. 2. 3. 4. 5.

Lifestyle goals for healthy living

Goal	Why is this goal important to me?	How will I reward myself for achieving my goal?

PART IV
MENTAL
Self-Care

"

It's not the load that breaks you down; it's the way you

carry it.

Lena Horne

Mental self-care

Mental self-care involves activities that help declutter your mind and reduce your stress levels. It encompasses anything you do specifically to stimulate your mind and cultivate a healthy psyche. It can be learning new things, practicing mindfulness and creativity. There is no wrong way to take care of your mental health, as long as it makes you feel relaxed!

How to practice mental self-care

✦ *Give attention to things that are in your control.* While we can always be in charge of many situations in our life, it's also important to know that there will be situations that are totally beyond our control. When you form a habit of learning to accept what you can't change, you will be saving yourself unnecessary mental stress.

✦ *Learn new things.*

✦ *Make time for relaxation.*

✦ *Focus more on the present.*

✦ *Perform a random act of kindness.*

+ *Practice mindfulness.* If you find that you are finding it difficult to focus on a specific task and your mind keeps wondering unnecessary, mindfulness can be highly beneficial. Mindfulness refers to the ability to be totally aware, and fully focused on the present and what we are doing rather than being overwhelmed by the things going on around us.

+ *Make time to engage with positive friends and family.*

+ *Try deep breathing exercises.* Deep breathing exercises can lower your heart rate blood pressure and breathing rate.

+ *Do something creative.*

+ *Do a digital detox.*

+ *Focus on positivity.*

+ *Stop to enjoy small aspects of the day.* Take time for personal reflection to notice your inner experiences, thoughts, and feelings.

+ *Cultivate self-awareness through things such as journalling.*

+ *Turn off your email and work phone outside of work hours.*

Self assessment

The purpose of this assessment is to build up an accurate picture of your needs. At the end of this assessment is a little box where you can note down the aspects you'd like to improve upon and how you plan to do it.

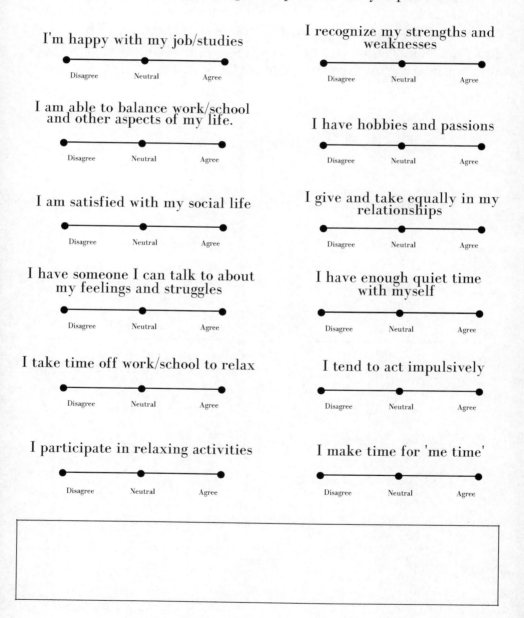

I'm happy with my job/studies

Disagree   Neutral   Agree

I recognize my strengths and weaknesses

Disagree   Neutral   Agree

I am able to balance work/school and other aspects of my life.

Disagree   Neutral   Agree

I have hobbies and passions

Disagree   Neutral   Agree

I am satisfied with my social life

Disagree   Neutral   Agree

I give and take equally in my relationships

Disagree   Neutral   Agree

I have someone I can talk to about my feelings and struggles

Disagree   Neutral   Agree

I have enough quiet time with myself

Disagree   Neutral   Agree

I take time off work/school to relax

Disagree   Neutral   Agree

I tend to act impulsively

Disagree   Neutral   Agree

I participate in relaxing activities

Disagree   Neutral   Agree

I make time for 'me time'

Disagree   Neutral   Agree

Wheel of life

This exercise is designed to take a snapshot of the current situation across variety of categories. This way you have an idea what you're happy with and what needs some extra work. The way you to do this is simple - First just give a rating from 1 to 10 in each category, one being you're totally unsatisfied and ten means that you're over the moon. Then on the next page, fill out what you're happy with and why and what needs some work and how you think you can improve the situation.

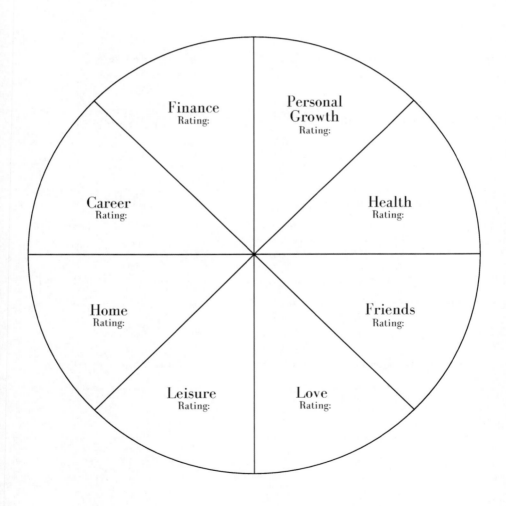

Wheel of life

Fill out what you're happy with and why and what needs some work and how you think you can improve the situation.

Career	Finance
Friends	Love
Personal Growth	Health
Leisure	Home

Core needs

Below is a list of common psychological and material needs . Go over the list to identify the needs that are important to you. There's no limit on how many you can select! If there's some other need that's not on the list, feel free to add it. After you've identified the needs, answer the questions on the next page and clarify what each of the needs means to you (since it can be very personal) and what actions can you take to fulfill it.

adventure	getting noticed	free time
accepted by others	feeling worthy	being loved
achieving success	being valued	getting attention
belonging	make people happy	feeling relaxed
being admired	make people laugh	personal growth
being right	intimacy	being useful
being in control	feeling love	being in control
creativity	order	being included
empowered	feeling safe	supported by others
frienship	having fun	
family	being wealthy	being independent
spiritual fulfillment	being recognized	feeling needed
stability	fulfilling work	being unique
status	expressing yourself	
power	feeling alive	
being respected	self development	

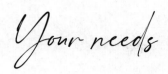

Your needs

Write down your needs and what do these mean do you?

....
....
....
....
....
....
....

What steps can you take to fulfill these needs?

....
....
....
....
....
....
....
....
....
....

Feelings wheel

Use the feelings wheel below to help you identify the emotional space you often occupy.

On the next page you'll be able to analyze more deeply why is it that you're experiencing certain emotions and what are the triggers.

Feelings wheel with the following segments:

SAD: Lacking, Wounded, Confused, Depressed, Isolated, Deserted, Lonely, Upset, Hurt

MAD: Contentious, Furious, Distressed, Frustrated, Irritated, Jealous, Hateful, Annoyed, Angry

HAPPY: Hopeful, Optimistic, Eager, Cheerful, Enthusiastic, Peaceful, Relaxed, Calm, Joyful

SCARED: Fearful, Agitated, Worried, Overwhelmed, Insecure, Defenseless, Powerless, Helpless, Anxious

Your feelings

What are the recurring emotion you're constantly feeling?

....

....

....

....

What are the main triggers for these emotion? (Certain people, places, situations etc.) Why do you think these triggers have such an impact?

....

....

....

....

How are these emotions beneficial for you and how are they holding you back? What actions can you take to start wheeling more empowering emotions and neutralize the triggers for negative emotions?

....

....

....

....

....

Taking responsibility for your own actions, emotions and current situation is the first step toward breaking out of old patterns and changing your life for the better. This is because all the things that you actually take responsibility (even if you're not directly to be blamed) for are the things that you can change, or if you can't change them, you can improve them going forward.

By answering the following questions, you gain some insight into how you can take more responsibility of the things that are holding you back. If you do not accept personal responsibility then you're approaching the problem as a victim - which means you can't do anything about it - which is counterproductive.

Write down your problem/s.

....

....

....

....

....

....

....

....

....

....

How am I responsible for this problem? Have I made some bad choices? Have I tried everything that's in my power to improve things? (if you have, count the things you've actually done)

....
....
....
....

If you solve this problem, how would your life (or the life of others) improve? Is this problem worth solving?

....
....
....
....
....

What can I do to start making things better? What little steps can I start making today to start improving the situation?

....
....
....
....
....

Accountability

How would taking responsibility for my relationships look like?
What steps must I take? How would this improve my life?

....

....

....

....

How would taking responsibility for my finances look like? What
steps must I take? How would this improve my life?

....

....

....

....

....

How would taking responsibility for my career look like? What
steps must I take? How would this improve my life?

....

....

....

....

How would taking responsibility for my health look like? What steps must I take? How would this improve my life?

....
....
....
....
....
....
....
....
....
....

How would taking responsibility for my wellbeing look like? What steps must I take? How would this improve my life?

....
....
....
....
....
....
....

Growth vs fixed mindset

Often times making progress with some problem starts with a simple shift in mindset. According to researcher Carol Dweck, there are two types of mindsets - fixed mindset and growth mindset. The former means that you believe that some quality or trait (intelligence for example) is innate and you have what you were given by nature. The essence of the latter however is that you can improve on any quality as long as you put in the effort. Therefore with growth mindset you're much more likely to take action and actually get something done. Below are some examples of growth vs fixed mindset.

Growth mindset

Challenges
Challenges are a way for me to get better

Desires
I'll try new things

Skills
I can always improve

Obstacles
I'll change my approach until I succeed

Success of others
Maybe I have something to learn from their success

Criticism
I can learn from the feedback I receive

Fixed mindset

Challenges
I try to avoid challenges so I don't look stupid

Desires
I'll just stick to what I know

Skills
I'm either good at it or not. If I'm not, it's okay.

Obstacles
I'm just not good at it and thats the way it is.

Success of others
It's unfair that they're succeeding and I'm not.

Criticism
I feel threatened by the criticism I get.

Working on my mindset

In this exercise try to identify your own mindset in a variety of categories and then write down what would be more productive mode of thinking instead (by productive we mean anything that will make you take action and actively work on a solution rather than just accept things as they are). On the next page you can also identify your own unique limiting beliefs and how you could reframe them.

How do I react to challenges & how can I improve?

....
....
....
....

How do I react to criticism & how can I improve?

....
....
....
....

How do I react when I don't know what to do?

....
....
....

Am I taking responsibility for my own actions and current situation in life? If yes/no, how so? Is this helping me to get forward and how?

....

....

....

....

....

....

....

....

....

....

....

....

....

....

....

....

....

....

....

....

Limiting beliefs

In this section, try to identify other beliefs that are holding you back and how you can reframe them to be more productive.

For example you may have been taught when you were little that "money does not grow on trees". While it's true in a sense, more productive way of thinking would be that "I will be rewarded for the value I provide for others - the more I give, the more I will receive".

Current belief

Better alternative

Current belief

Better alternative

"

Your willingness to look at your darkness is what

empowers you to

change.

Iyanla Vanzant

Limiting beliefs

A belief that is holding you back:

....

....

....

....

Where did this belief come from?

....

....

....

How is this belief harmful?

....

....

....

What is a better alternative for this belief?

....

....

....

....

Fear setting

This exercise is loosely based on a section from Tim Ferriss's "4 Hour Work Week" and involves thinking about the worst possible outcomes of an action you know you should take but are too afraid to execute. This allows you to write three categories for each action.

First the worst possible outcomes.

Second how to prevent these outcomes.

And third, when these outcome really come to pass, how you can mitigate the adverse effects. This should help you come to a realization that the things that you're afraid of are really not that bad.

The final category to fill out is what would happen long term if you decided not take take the desired action (this helps you use a proverbial stick on yourself to push yourself towards taking action).

Don't let the fear of what could happen make nothing happen.

Doe Zantamata

What action do you wish to take		
The worst outcomes	How to prevent	How to repair

What will happen long term (1 year, 5 years, 10 years) if I don't take this action?

Taking action

I am going to: (ex. build a 6 figure passion business)

....

....

....

....

What limiting beliefs do I have to overcome to achieve this: (ex. I can't quit my current job because I can't pay for my rent.)

....

....

....

What steps do I have to take to get started: (ex. start sharing my products on Etsy)

....

....

....

What tools do I need to get started:

....

....

....

....

Why am I doing this: (ex. I'm doing this because life is too short to not take chances)

....

....

....

....

....

....

....

....

....

....

I am grateful for: (ex. the opportunity to pursue my dream)

....

....

....

....

....

....

....

....

Fighting fear

What makes you feel nervous or scared?

....

....

....

....

What can be done?

....

....

....

What do you think about when you are nervous or scared?

....

....

....

What is something you can do to feel better next time?

....

....

....

....

478
Breathing technique

This breathing technique can aid relaxation and sleep. Start by sitting or lying in a comfortable position.

Repeat this technique 4 times.

4

Breathe in through your nose.

4 seconds.

7

Hold your breath.

7 seconds.

8

Breathe in through your mouth.

8 seconds.

Worry exploration

What are you worried about?

....

....

....

....

What are some clues that show your worry will not come true?

....

....

....

If your worry does not come true, what will probably happen instead?

....

....

....

The worst that can happen is ...

....

....

....

Positive experiences

Write briefly about the times when you displayed each of the following qualities.

Courage

....

Kindness

....

Selflessness

....

Love

....

Excitement

....

Happiness

....

Creative

....

Calm

....

PART V
A MONTH OF
Self-Care

Care about yourself

Do something for yourself everyday. Each day color the heart.

Important questions

What do you want to achieve emotionally in the next month?

....

....

....

....

What do you want to achieve spiritually in the next month?

....

....

....

....

What do you want to achieve physically in the next month?

....

....

....

....

What do you want to achieve mentally in the next month?

....

....

....

....

"

When I'm tired, I rest. I say,

'I can't be a superwoman today.'

Jada Pinkett Smith

Monthly overview

My focus this month... (e.g. is to live in the present moment)

....

....

This month I commit to... (e.g. eating protein and veg with each meal)

1. ....

2. ....

3. ....

Affirmations for this month (e.g. I am going to get everything I want in this month)

1. ....

2. ....

3. ....

Monthly intentions (e.g. Get more comfortable saying "NO")

....

....

....

....

Dream self

The person I want to be (e.g. motivated, healthy, at peace, determined)

....

....

Negative blockers (e.g. toxic and negative people in my life)

....

....

How I can overcome them (e.g. cut them out)

....

....

Positive habits to help me get there (e.g. stop caring so much what others think/say)

....

....

....

Positive mantras

I am ....

I feel ....

I have ....

Monthly self-care goals

TOP 3 GOALS	ACTION STEPS TO TAKE

GOAL 1	1.
	2.
YOUR WHY	3.
	4.
REWARD	5.

GOAL 2	1.
	2.
YOUR WHY	3.
	4.
REWARD	5.

GOAL 3	1.
	2.
YOUR WHY	3.
	4.
REWARD	5.

Self-care plan

Things I can do when I'm sad

....

....

....

Things I can do when I'm bored

....

....

....

Things I'm looking forward to

....

....

....

Things I want to manifest into my life

....

....

....

Next exciting things on my bucket list

....

....

....

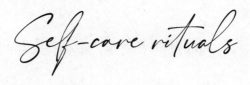

Self-care rituals

Morning rituals (ex. Green smoothie, lemon water, morning yoga)

....

....

....

....

....

....

....

....

Evening rituals (ex. Take a bath, light a candle, read)

....

....

....

....

....

....

....

....

Monthly habit tracker

Monthly habits:

COLOR
☐ _____
☐ _____
☐ _____
☐ _____
☐ _____
☐ _____
☐ _____

Monthly mood tracker

With our Mood Tracker, you may track your triggers, look at your ups and downs, and give yourself permission to feel in order to better understand your anxiety, aid in stress reduction and become a happier person in general. You may be able to identify events or periods when your mood rises or falls by recording your emotions. Such occurrences are frequently referred to as triggers. For example, if you observe that you become depressed whenever you visit your parents, it's significant knowledge that you can use to better understand yourself.

COLOR YOUR MOOD

30 DAY
Self-care challenge

It's time for some rest, relaxation, and good old self-care! This 30 day self-care challenge will give you many different ways to improve all areas of your life. If you need a refresh but are unsure where to start, this self-care challenge will walk you through it all.

DAY 1	DAY 2	DAY 3	DAY 4	DAY 5
Take a walk without your phone	Stretch for 15 minutes in the morning	Declutter your space	Call someone you love	Listen to a podcast
DAY 6	DAY 7	DAY 8	DAY 9	DAY 10
Learn to cook a new recipe	Listen to your favorite song	Practice deep breathing	Try an online workout	Read a book for 20 minutes
DAY 11	DAY 12	DAY 13	DAY 14	DAY 15
Go to bed 30 minutes earlier	Make your favorite meal	Buy yourself something nice	Write down your thoughts	Take a long shower or bath
DAY 16	DAY 17	DAY 18	DAY 19	DAY 20
Have a home spa day	Create a vision board	Read inspirational quotes	Do a hair mask	Take yourself out to eat
DAY 21	DAY 22	DAY 23	DAY 24	DAY 25
Do yoga	Write a list of compliments to yourself	Light a candle	Watch the sunrise or sunset	Spend quality time with a loved one
DAY 26	DAY 27	DAY 28	DAY 29	DAY 30
Spend some time in the sun	Meditate for 10 minutes	Unplug from social media	Take a nap	Pay it forward

30 DAY
Self-care challenge

If our self-care challenge is not exactly what you need then you can create your own challenge. You can personalize your self-care challenge to be what will help you reset and find your inner peace.

DAY 1	DAY 2	DAY 3	DAY 4	DAY 5
DAY 6	DAY 7	DAY 8	DAY 9	DAY 10
DAY 11	DAY 12	DAY 13	DAY 14	DAY 15
DAY 16	DAY 17	DAY 18	DAY 19	DAY 20
DAY 21	DAY 22	DAY 23	DAY 24	DAY 25
DAY 26	DAY 27	DAY 28	DAY 29	DAY 30

Monthly water challenge

Stay healthy — stay hydrated! Water tracker helps you to drink more water and stay hydrated!

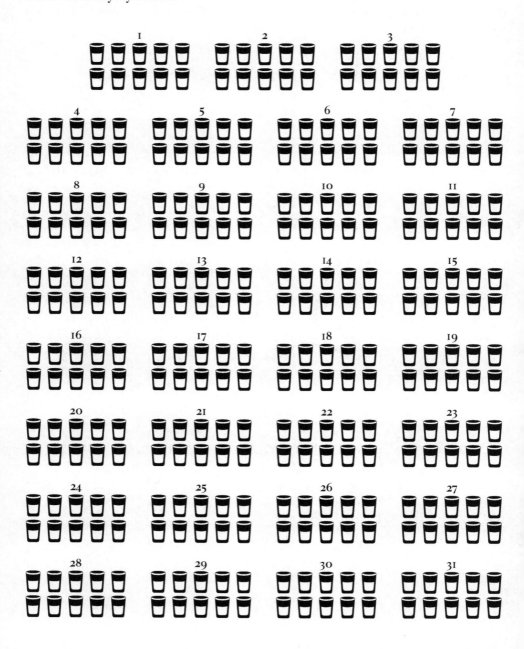

Body measurements tracker

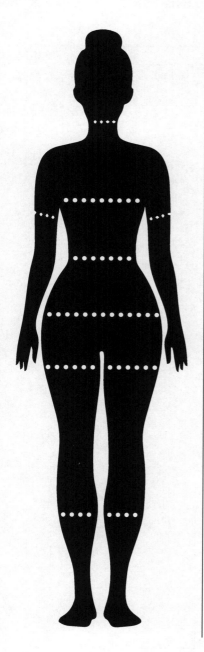

ARMS

WEEK 1	
WEEK 2	
WEEK 3	
WEEK 4	

HIPS

WEEK 1	
WEEK 2	
WEEK 3	
WEEK 4	

WAIST

WEEK 1	
WEEK 2	
WEEK 3	
WEEK 4	

LEGS

WEEK 1	
WEEK 2	
WEEK 3	
WEEK 4	

Sleep tracker

Track and fill in your sleeping hours each day and be surprised at your pattern at the end of the month!

DATE	HOURS OF SLEEP												ENERGY
DAY	1	2	3	4	5	6	7	8	9	10	11	12	★ ★ ★ ★ ★

Monthly Medications, Supplements, Vitamins Tracker

Product	1	2	3	4	5	6	7	8	9	10	11	12	13	14	15	16	17	18	19	20	21	22	23	24	25	26	27	28	29	30	31

DATE: ____ / ____ / ____   M   T   W   T   F   S   S

TODAY I WANT TO FEEL: ....

AN INTENTION FOR THE DAY: ....

DAILY AFFIRMATION: ....

TO DO

6:00AM ....

7:00AM ....

8:00AM ....

9:00AM ....

10:00AM ....

11:00AM ....

12:00PM ....

1:00PM ....

2:00PM ....

3:00PM ....

4:00PM ....

5:00PM ....

6:00PM ....

7:00PM ....

8:00PM ....

9:00PM ....

10:00PM ....

MOOD

MEAL PLAN

WATER   ◊ ◊ ◊ ◊ ◊ ◊ ◊ ◊ ◊

BREAKFAST ....

LUNCH ....

DINNER ....

EXERCISE

☐ ....

☐ ....

☐ ....

☐ ....

MAIN GOALS

☐ ....

☐ ....

☐ ....

☐ ....

SELF-CARE	TODAY'S WINS	TODAY I'M GRATEFUL FOR
♡	☐	....
♡	☐	....
♡	☐	....
♡	☐	....

PHYSICALLY, EMOTIONALLY AND MENTALLY I FELT

☐ Relaxed   ☐ Joyful   ☐ Loved   ☐ Vulnerable   ☐ Mad
☐ Energized   ☐ Grateful   ☐ Peaceful   ☐ Misunderstood   ☐ Sore
☐ Well-rested ☐ Optimistic   ☐ Valued   ☐ Stressed   ☐ Weak
☐ Inspired   ☐ Excited   ☐ Unmotivated   ☐ Irritated   ☐ Upset
☐ Motivated   ☐ Fulfilled   ☐ Nervous   ☐ Depressed   ☐ Tired
☐ Creative   ☐ Hopeful   ☐ Frustrated   ☐ Anxious   ☐ Drained

THINGS THAT WERE FUN OR RELAXING TODAY

....

....

THINGS THAT WERE TOUGH OR STRESSFUL TODAY

....

....

KIND THINGS I DID FOR MYSELF TODAY

....

....

WHAT WAS MY FAVORITE PART OF TODAY?

....

....

HOW CAN I MAKE TOMORROW BETTER?

....

....

NOTES AND REFLECTIONS

"

Sometimes you've got to let
everything go -

purge yourself.

If you are unhappy with anything,

get rid of it.

Tina Turner

DAILY REFLECTION

How am I communicating my needs with the people in my life?

....
....
....
....
....
....
....
....
....
....
....
....
....
....
....
....
....
....
....
....
....
....

DATE: ____ / ____ / ____   M   T   W   T   F   S   S

TODAY I WANT TO FEEL: ....

AN INTENTION FOR THE DAY: ....

DAILY AFFIRMATION: ....

TO DO

6:00AM ....

7:00AM ....

8:00AM ....

9:00AM ....

10:00AM ....

11:00AM ....

12:00PM ....

1:00PM ....

2:00PM ....

3:00PM ....

4:00PM ....

5:00PM ....

6:00PM ....

7:00PM ....

8:00PM ....

9:00PM ....

10:00PM ....

MOOD

MEAL PLAN

WATER   ☌ ☌ ☌ ☌ ☌ ☌ ☌ ☌

BREAKFAST ....

LUNCH ....

DINNER ....

EXERCISE

☐ ....

☐ ....

☐ ....

☐ ....

MAIN GOALS

☐ ....

☐ ....

☐ ....

☐ ....

SELF-CARE	TODAY'S WINS	TODAY I'M GRATEFUL FOR
♡	☐	....
♡	☐	....
♡	☐	....
♡	☐	....

PHYSICALLY, EMOTIONALLY AND MENTALLY I FELT

☐ Relaxed	☐ Joyful	☐ Loved	☐ Vulnerable	☐ Mad
☐ Energized	☐ Grateful	☐ Peaceful	☐ Misunderstood	☐ Sore
☐ Well-rested	☐ Optimistic	☐ Valued	☐ Stressed	☐ Weak
☐ Inspired	☐ Excited	☐ Unmotivated	☐ Irritated	☐ Upset
☐ Motivated	☐ Fulfilled	☐ Nervous	☐ Depressed	☐ Tired
☐ Creative	☐ Hopeful	☐ Frustrated	☐ Anxious	☐ Drained

THINGS THAT WERE FUN OR RELAXING TODAY

....

....

THINGS THAT WERE TOUGH OR STRESSFUL TODAY

....

....

KIND THINGS I DID FOR MYSELF TODAY

....

....

WHAT WAS MY FAVORITE PART OF TODAY?

....

....

HOW CAN I MAKE TOMORROW BETTER?

....

....

NOTES AND REFLECTIONS

Read out loud

I RECLAIM MY OWN POWER.

I EASILY OVERCOME
STRESSFUL SITUATIONS.

MY PEACE IS MY POWER.

What helps me slow down and feel more present?

....
....
....
....
....
....
....
....
....
....
....
....
....
....
....
....
....
....
....
....
....
....
....
....
....

DATE: ____ / ____ / ____   M   T   W   T   F   S   S

TODODAY I WANT TO FEEL: ....

AN INTENTION FOR THE DAY: ....

DAILY AFFIRMATION: ....

TO DO

6:00AM ....

7:00AM ....

8:00AM ....

9:00AM ....

10:00AM ....

11:00AM ....

12:00PM ....

1:00PM ....

2:00PM ....

3:00PM ....

4:00PM ....

5:00PM ....

6:00PM ....

7:00PM ....

8:00PM ....

9:00PM ....

10:00PM ....

MOOD

MEAL PLAN

WATER   ◊ ◊ ◊ ◊ ◊ ◊ ◊ ◊

BREAKFAST ....

LUNCH ....

DINNER ....

EXERCISE

☐ ....

☐ ....

☐ ....

☐ ....

MAIN GOALS

☐ ....

☐ ....

☐ ....

☐ ....

SELF-CARE	TODAY'S WINS	TODAY I'M GRATEFUL FOR
♡	☐	....
♡	☐	....
♡	☐	....
♡	☐	....

PHYSICALLY, EMOTIONALLY AND MENTALLY I FELT

- [ ] Relaxed
- [ ] Joyful
- [ ] Loved
- [ ] Vulnerable
- [ ] Mad
- [ ] Energized
- [ ] Grateful
- [ ] Peaceful
- [ ] Misunderstood
- [ ] Sore
- [ ] Well-rested
- [ ] Optimistic
- [ ] Valued
- [ ] Stressed
- [ ] Weak
- [ ] Inspired
- [ ] Excited
- [ ] Unmotivated
- [ ] Irritated
- [ ] Upset
- [ ] Motivated
- [ ] Fulfilled
- [ ] Nervous
- [ ] Depressed
- [ ] Tired
- [ ] Creative
- [ ] Hopeful
- [ ] Frustrated
- [ ] Anxious
- [ ] Drained

THINGS THAT WERE FUN OR RELAXING TODAY

THINGS THAT WERE TOUGH OR STRESSFUL TODAY

KIND THINGS I DID FOR MYSELF TODAY

WHAT WAS MY FAVORITE PART OF TODAY?

HOW CAN I MAKE TOMORROW BETTER?

NOTES AND REFLECTIONS

Write it down

I AM A BROWN SKIN BEAUTY WHO KNOWS HER WORTH.

1.

2.

3.

4.

5.

6.

7.

8.

9.

10.

If I received $5,000 that I had to spend on myself, I would...

....
....
....
....
....
....
....
....
....
....
....
....
....
....
....
....
....
....
....
....
....

DATE: ____ / ____ / ____   M   T   W   T   F   S   S

TODAY I WANT TO FEEL: ....

AN INTENTION FOR THE DAY: ....

DAILY AFFIRMATION: ....

TO DO

6:00AM	....
7:00AM	....
8:00AM	....
9:00AM	....
10:00AM	....
11:00AM	....
12:00PM	....
1:00PM	....
2:00PM	....
3:00PM	....
4:00PM	....
5:00PM	....
6:00PM	....
7:00PM	....
8:00PM	....
9:00PM	....
10:00PM	....

MOOD

MEAL PLAN

WATER   ⬡ ⬡ ⬡ ⬡ ⬡ ⬡ ⬡ ⬡

BREAKFAST ....

LUNCH ....

DINNER ....

EXERCISE

☐ ....
☐ ....
☐ ....
☐ ....

MAIN GOALS

☐ ....
☐ ....
☐ ....
☐ ....

SELF-CARE	TODAY'S WINS	TODAY I'M GRATEFUL FOR
♡	☐	....
♡	☐	....
♡	☐	....
♡	☐	....

PHYSICALLY, EMOTIONALLY AND MENTALLY I FELT

☐ Relaxed	☐ Joyful	☐ Loved	☐ Vulnerable	☐ Mad
☐ Energized	☐ Grateful	☐ Peaceful	☐ Misunderstood	☐ Sore
☐ Well-rested	☐ Optimistic	☐ Valued	☐ Stressed	☐ Weak
☐ Inspired	☐ Excited	☐ Unmotivated	☐ Irritated	☐ Upset
☐ Motivated	☐ Fulfilled	☐ Nervous	☐ Depressed	☐ Tired
☐ Creative	☐ Hopeful	☐ Frustrated	☐ Anxious	☐ Drained

THINGS THAT WERE FUN OR RELAXING TODAY

....

....

THINGS THAT WERE TOUGH OR STRESSFUL TODAY

....

....

KIND THINGS I DID FOR MYSELF TODAY

....

....

WHAT WAS MY FAVORITE PART OF TODAY?

....

....

HOW CAN I MAKE TOMORROW BETTER?

....

....

NOTES AND REFLECTIONS

"

Speak up for yourself and what you believe in. You can still be an elegant woman and be

strong and powerful.

What am I doing that is distracting me from being with myself? How will making myself a priority positively impact my life?

....
....
....
....
....
....
....
....
....
....
....
....
....
....
....
....
....
....
....
....
....
....

DATE: ____ / ____ / ____   M   T   W   T   F   S   S

TODAY I WANT TO FEEL: ....

AN INTENTION FOR THE DAY: ....

DAILY AFFIRMATION: ....

TO DO

6:00AM ....
7:00AM ....
8:00AM ....
9:00AM ....
10:00AM ....
11:00AM ....
12:00PM ....
1:00PM ....
2:00PM ....
3:00PM ....
4:00PM ....
5:00PM ....
6:00PM ....
7:00PM ....
8:00PM ....
9:00PM ....
10:00PM ....

MOOD

MEAL PLAN

WATER   ⬭ ⬭ ⬭ ⬭ ⬭ ⬭ ⬭ ⬭

BREAKFAST ....
LUNCH ....
DINNER ....

EXERCISE

☐ ....
☐ ....
☐ ....
☐ ....

MAIN GOALS

☐ ....
☐ ....
☐ ....
☐ ....

SELF-CARE	TODAY'S WINS	TODAY I'M GRATEFUL FOR
♡	☐	....
♡	☐	....
♡	☐	....
♡	☐	....

PHYSICALLY, EMOTIONALLY AND MENTALLY I FELT

☐ Relaxed	☐ Joyful	☐ Loved	☐ Vulnerable	☐ Mad
☐ Energized	☐ Grateful	☐ Peaceful	☐ Misunderstood	☐ Sore
☐ Well-rested	☐ Optimistic	☐ Valued	☐ Stressed	☐ Weak
☐ Inspired	☐ Excited	☐ Unmotivated	☐ Irritated	☐ Upset
☐ Motivated	☐ Fulfilled	☐ Nervous	☐ Depressed	☐ Tired
☐ Creative	☐ Hopeful	☐ Frustrated	☐ Anxious	☐ Drained

THINGS THAT WERE FUN OR RELAXING TODAY

....

....

THINGS THAT WERE TOUGH OR STRESSFUL TODAY

....

....

KIND THINGS I DID FOR MYSELF TODAY

....

....

WHAT WAS MY FAVORITE PART OF TODAY?

....

....

HOW CAN I MAKE TOMORROW BETTER?

....

....

NOTES AND REFLECTIONS

Read out loud

I AM IN HARMONY AND
BALANCE WITH LIFE.

I DESERVE TO FEEL SAFE,
COMFORTABLE AND
CONFIDENT IN THIS BODY.

If I could make a living doing anything, what would it be?

....
....
....
....
....
....
....
....
....
....
....
....
....
....
....
....
....
....
....
....
....
....

DATE: ___ / ___ / ___   M   T   W   T   F   S   S

TODAY I WANT TO FEEL: ....

AN INTENTION FOR THE DAY: ....

DAILY AFFIRMATION: ....

TO DO

6:00AM ....
7:00AM ....
8:00AM ....
9:00AM ....
10:00AM ....
11:00AM ....
12:00PM ....
1:00PM ....
2:00PM ....
3:00PM ....
4:00PM ....
5:00PM ....
6:00PM ....
7:00PM ....
8:00PM ....
9:00PM ....
10:00PM ....

MOOD

MEAL PLAN

WATER   ○ ○ ○ ○ ○ ○ ○ ○

BREAKFAST ....
LUNCH   ....
DINNER   ....

EXERCISE

☐ ....
☐ ....
☐ ....
☐ ....

MAIN GOALS

☐ ....
☐ ....
☐ ....
☐ ....

SELF-CARE	TODAY'S WINS	TODAY I'M GRATEFUL FOR
♡	☐	....
♡	☐	....
♡	☐	....
♡	☐	....

PHYSICALLY, EMOTIONALLY AND MENTALLY I FELT

☐ Relaxed	☐ Joyful	☐ Loved	☐ Vulnerable	☐ Mad
☐ Energized	☐ Grateful	☐ Peaceful	☐ Misunderstood	☐ Sore
☐ Well-rested	☐ Optimistic	☐ Valued	☐ Stressed	☐ Weak
☐ Inspired	☐ Excited	☐ Unmotivated	☐ Irritated	☐ Upset
☐ Motivated	☐ Fulfilled	☐ Nervous	☐ Depressed	☐ Tired
☐ Creative	☐ Hopeful	☐ Frustrated	☐ Anxious	☐ Drained

THINGS THAT WERE FUN OR RELAXING TODAY

....

....

THINGS THAT WERE TOUGH OR STRESSFUL TODAY

....

....

KIND THINGS I DID FOR MYSELF TODAY

....

....

WHAT WAS MY FAVORITE PART OF TODAY?

....

....

HOW CAN I MAKE TOMORROW BETTER?

....

....

NOTES AND REFLECTIONS

Write it down

I ACCEPT MYSELF
THE WAY I AM.

1. _____

2. _____

3. _____

4. _____

5. _____

6. _____

7. _____

8. _____

9. _____

10. _____

What thought patterns are holding me back right now?

....
....
....
....
....
....
....
....
....
....
....
....
....
....
....
....
....
....
....
....
....
....
....
....

DATE: ___ / ___ / ___   M T W T F S S

TODAY I WANT TO FEEL: ....

AN INTENTION FOR THE DAY: ....

DAILY AFFIRMATION: ....

TO DO

6:00AM ....
7:00AM ....
8:00AM ....
9:00AM ....
10:00AM ....
11:00AM ....
12:00PM ....
1:00PM ....
2:00PM ....
3:00PM ....
4:00PM ....
5:00PM ....
6:00PM ....
7:00PM ....
8:00PM ....
9:00PM ....
10:00PM ....

MOOD

MEAL PLAN

WATER   ⬡ ⬡ ⬡ ⬡ ⬡ ⬡ ⬡ ⬡

BREAKFAST ....
LUNCH ....
DINNER ....

EXERCISE

☐ ....
☐ ....
☐ ....
☐ ....

MAIN GOALS

☐ ....
☐ ....
☐ ....
☐ ....

SELF-CARE	TODAY'S WINS	TODAY I'M GRATEFUL FOR
♡	☐	....
♡	☐	....
♡	☐	....
♡	☐	....

PHYSICALLY, EMOTIONALLY AND MENTALLY I FELT

☐ Relaxed	☐ Joyful	☐ Loved	☐ Vulnerable	☐ Mad
☐ Energized	☐ Grateful	☐ Peaceful	☐ Misunderstood	☐ Sore
☐ Well-rested	☐ Optimistic	☐ Valued	☐ Stressed	☐ Weak
☐ Inspired	☐ Excited	☐ Unmotivated	☐ Irritated	☐ Upset
☐ Motivated	☐ Fulfilled	☐ Nervous	☐ Depressed	☐ Tired
☐ Creative	☐ Hopeful	☐ Frustrated	☐ Anxious	☐ Drained

THINGS THAT WERE FUN OR RELAXING TODAY

....

....

THINGS THAT WERE TOUGH OR STRESSFUL TODAY

....

....

KIND THINGS I DID FOR MYSELF TODAY

....

....

WHAT WAS MY FAVORITE PART OF TODAY?

....

....

HOW CAN I MAKE TOMORROW BETTER?

....

....

NOTES AND REFLECTIONS

"

You are

your best thing.

Toni Morrison

When was a time I felt really happy?
Write about a happy time.

....
....
....
....
....
....
....
....
....
....
....
....
....
....
....
....
....
....
....
....
....
....
....

DATE: ___ / ___ / ___   M   T   W   T   F   S   S

TODAY I WANT TO FEEL: ....

AN INTENTION FOR THE DAY: ....

DAILY AFFIRMATION: ....

TO DO

6:00AM ....
7:00AM ....
8:00AM ....
9:00AM ....
10:00AM ....
11:00AM ....
12:00PM ....
1:00PM ....
2:00PM ....
3:00PM ....
4:00PM ....
5:00PM ....
6:00PM ....
7:00PM ....
8:00PM ....
9:00PM ....
10:00PM ....

MOOD

MEAL PLAN

WATER   △ △ △ △ △ △ △ △
BREAKFAST ....
LUNCH ....
DINNER ....

EXERCISE

☐ ....
☐ ....
☐ ....
☐ ....

MAIN GOALS

☐ ....
☐ ....
☐ ....
☐ ....

SELF-CARE	TODAY'S WINS	TODAY I'M GRATEFUL FOR
♡	☐	....
♡	☐	....
♡	☐	....
♡	☐	....

PHYSICALLY, EMOTIONALLY AND MENTALLY I FELT

☐ Relaxed	☐ Joyful	☐ Loved	☐ Vulnerable	☐ Mad
☐ Energized	☐ Grateful	☐ Peaceful	☐ Misunderstood	☐ Sore
☐ Well-rested	☐ Optimistic	☐ Valued	☐ Stressed	☐ Weak
☐ Inspired	☐ Excited	☐ Unmotivated	☐ Irritated	☐ Upset
☐ Motivated	☐ Fulfilled	☐ Nervous	☐ Depressed	☐ Tired
☐ Creative	☐ Hopeful	☐ Frustrated	☐ Anxious	☐ Drained

THINGS THAT WERE FUN OR RELAXING TODAY

....

....

THINGS THAT WERE TOUGH OR STRESSFUL TODAY

....

....

KIND THINGS I DID FOR MYSELF TODAY

....

....

WHAT WAS MY FAVORITE PART OF TODAY?

....

....

HOW CAN I MAKE TOMORROW BETTER?

....

....

NOTES AND REFLECTIONS

Read out loud

I AM LOVED FOR EXACTLY WHO I AM.

I AM PERFECT AND COMPLETE JUST
THE WAY I AM.

I AM ENOUGH.

How can I show myself more love?

....
....
....
....
....
....
....
....
....
....
....
....
....
....
....
....
....
....
....
....
....
....
....

DATE: ___ / ___ / ___   M   T   W   T   F   S   S

TODAY I WANT TO FEEL: ....

AN INTENTION FOR THE DAY: ....

DAILY AFFIRMATION: ....

TO DO

6:00AM ....

7:00AM ....

8:00AM ....

9:00AM ....

10:00AM ....

11:00AM ....

12:00PM ....

1:00PM ....

2:00PM ....

3:00PM ....

4:00PM ....

5:00PM ....

6:00PM ....

7:00PM ....

8:00PM ....

9:00PM ....

10:00PM ....

MOOD

MEAL PLAN

WATER   ○ ○ ○ ○ ○ ○ ○ ○ ○

BREAKFAST ....

LUNCH ....

DINNER ....

EXERCISE

☐ ....

☐ ....

☐ ....

☐ ....

MAIN GOALS

☐ ....

☐ ....

☐ ....

☐ ....

SELF-CARE	TODAY'S WINS	TODAY I'M GRATEFUL FOR
♡	☐	....
♡	☐	....
♡	☐	....
♡	☐	....

PHYSICALLY, EMOTIONALLY AND MENTALLY I FELT

☐ Relaxed   ☐ Joyful   ☐ Loved   ☐ Vulnerable   ☐ Mad

☐ Energized   ☐ Grateful   ☐ Peaceful   ☐ Misunderstood   ☐ Sore

☐ Well-rested ☐ Optimistic   ☐ Valued   ☐ Stressed   ☐ Weak

☐ Inspired   ☐ Excited   ☐ Unmotivated   ☐ Irritated   ☐ Upset

☐ Motivated   ☐ Fulfilled   ☐ Nervous   ☐ Depressed   ☐ Tired

☐ Creative   ☐ Hopeful   ☐ Frustrated   ☐ Anxious   ☐ Drained

THINGS THAT WERE FUN OR RELAXING TODAY

....

....

THINGS THAT WERE TOUGH OR STRESSFUL TODAY

....

....

KIND THINGS I DID FOR MYSELF TODAY

....

....

WHAT WAS MY FAVORITE PART OF TODAY?

....

....

HOW CAN I MAKE TOMORROW BETTER?

....

....

NOTES AND REFLECTIONS

I AM POWERFUL, MELANATED, AND CAPABLE OF RUNNING MY WORLD.

1. _____

2. _____

3. _____

4. _____

5. _____

6. _____

7. _____

8. _____

9. _____

10. _____

What does my dream life look like? What's my ultimate goal in life?

....
....
....
....
....
....
....
....
....
....
....
....
....
....
....
....
....
....
....
....
....
....
....
....
....

DATE: ____ / ____ / ____   M   T   W   T   F   S   S

TODAY I WANT TO FEEL: ....

AN INTENTION FOR THE DAY: ....

DAILY AFFIRMATION: ....

TO DO

6:00AM ....

7:00AM ....

8:00AM ....

9:00AM ....

10:00AM ....

11:00AM ....

12:00PM ....

1:00PM ....

2:00PM ....

3:00PM ....

4:00PM ....

5:00PM ....

6:00PM ....

7:00PM ....

8:00PM ....

9:00PM ....

10:00PM ....

MOOD

MEAL PLAN

WATER   ⬦ ⬦ ⬦ ⬦ ⬦ ⬦ ⬦ ⬦

BREAKFAST ....

LUNCH ....

DINNER ....

EXERCISE

☐ ....

☐ ....

☐ ....

☐ ....

MAIN GOALS

☐ ....

☐ ....

☐ ....

☐ ....

SELF-CARE	TODAY'S WINS	TODAY I'M GRATEFUL FOR
♡	☐	....
♡	☐	....
♡	☐	....
♡	☐	....

PHYSICALLY, EMOTIONALLY AND MENTALLY I FELT

☐ Relaxed	☐ Joyful	☐ Loved	☐ Vulnerable	☐ Mad
☐ Energized	☐ Grateful	☐ Peaceful	☐ Misunderstood	☐ Sore
☐ Well-rested	☐ Optimistic	☐ Valued	☐ Stressed	☐ Weak
☐ Inspired	☐ Excited	☐ Unmotivated	☐ Irritated	☐ Upset
☐ Motivated	☐ Fulfilled	☐ Nervous	☐ Depressed	☐ Tired
☐ Creative	☐ Hopeful	☐ Frustrated	☐ Anxious	☐ Drained

THINGS THAT WERE FUN OR RELAXING TODAY

....

....

THINGS THAT WERE TOUGH OR STRESSFUL TODAY

....

....

KIND THINGS I DID FOR MYSELF TODAY

....

....

WHAT WAS MY FAVORITE PART OF TODAY?

....

....

HOW CAN I MAKE TOMORROW BETTER?

....

....

NOTES AND REFLECTIONS

"

Self-esteem means knowing

you are the

dream.

Oprah Winfrey

What do I need to be more at peace with myself?

DATE: ___/___/___   M   T   W   T   F   S   S

TODAY I WANT TO FEEL: ....

AN INTENTION FOR THE DAY: ....

DAILY AFFIRMATION: ....

TO DO

6:00AM ....

7:00AM ....

8:00AM ....

9:00AM ....

10:00AM ....

11:00AM ....

12:00PM ....

1:00PM ....

2:00PM ....

3:00PM ....

4:00PM ....

5:00PM ....

6:00PM ....

7:00PM ....

8:00PM ....

9:00PM ....

10:00PM ....

MOOD

MEAL PLAN

WATER ◇ ◇ ◇ ◇ ◇ ◇ ◇ ◇ ◇

BREAKFAST ....

LUNCH ....

DINNER ....

EXERCISE

☐ ....

☐ ....

☐ ....

☐ ....

MAIN GOALS

☐ ....

☐ ....

☐ ....

☐ ....

SELF-CARE	TODAY'S WINS	TODAY I'M GRATEFUL FOR
♡	☐	....
♡	☐	....
♡	☐	....
♡	☐	....

PHYSICALLY, EMOTIONALLY AND MENTALLY I FELT

- [ ] Relaxed
- [ ] Energized
- [ ] Well-rested
- [ ] Inspired
- [ ] Motivated
- [ ] Creative

- [ ] Joyful
- [ ] Grateful
- [ ] Optimistic
- [ ] Excited
- [ ] Fulfilled
- [ ] Hopeful

- [ ] Loved
- [ ] Peaceful
- [ ] Valued
- [ ] Unmotivated
- [ ] Nervous
- [ ] Frustrated

- [ ] Vulnerable
- [ ] Misunderstood
- [ ] Stressed
- [ ] Irritated
- [ ] Depressed
- [ ] Anxious

- [ ] Mad
- [ ] Sore
- [ ] Weak
- [ ] Upset
- [ ] Tired
- [ ] Drained

THINGS THAT WERE FUN OR RELAXING TODAY

....

....

THINGS THAT WERE TOUGH OR STRESSFUL TODAY

....

....

KIND THINGS I DID FOR MYSELF TODAY

....

....

WHAT WAS MY FAVORITE PART OF TODAY?

....

....

HOW CAN I MAKE TOMORROW BETTER?

....

....

NOTES AND REFLECTIONS

Read out loud

I AM GRATEFUL TO BE LIVING IN THIS DIVINE FEMALE BODY.

What do I love about my life? When am I the happiest version of me?

....
....
....
....
....
....
....
....
....
....
....
....
....
....
....
....
....
....
....
....
....
....
....

DATE: ____ / ____ / ____   M   T   W   T   F   S   S

TODAY I WANT TO FEEL: ....

AN INTENTION FOR THE DAY: ....

DAILY AFFIRMATION: ....

TO DO

6:00AM	....
7:00AM	....
8:00AM	....
9:00AM	....
10:00AM	....
11:00AM	....
12:00PM	....
1:00PM	....
2:00PM	....
3:00PM	....
4:00PM	....
5:00PM	....
6:00PM	....
7:00PM	....
8:00PM	....
9:00PM	....
10:00PM	....

MOOD

MEAL PLAN

WATER ◊ ◊ ◊ ◊ ◊ ◊ ◊ ◊ ◊

BREAKFAST ....

LUNCH ....

DINNER ....

EXERCISE

☐ ....
☐ ....
☐ ....
☐ ....

MAIN GOALS

☐ ....
☐ ....
☐ ....
☐ ....

SELF-CARE	TODAY'S WINS	TODAY I'M GRATEFUL FOR
♡	☐	....
♡	☐	....
♡	☐	....
♡	☐	....

PHYSICALLY, EMOTIONALLY AND MENTALLY I FELT

- [ ] Relaxed
- [ ] Joyful
- [ ] Loved
- [ ] Vulnerable
- [ ] Mad
- [ ] Energized
- [ ] Grateful
- [ ] Peaceful
- [ ] Misunderstood
- [ ] Sore
- [ ] Well-rested
- [ ] Optimistic
- [ ] Valued
- [ ] Stressed
- [ ] Weak
- [ ] Inspired
- [ ] Excited
- [ ] Unmotivated
- [ ] Irritated
- [ ] Upset
- [ ] Motivated
- [ ] Fulfilled
- [ ] Nervous
- [ ] Depressed
- [ ] Tired
- [ ] Creative
- [ ] Hopeful
- [ ] Frustrated
- [ ] Anxious
- [ ] Drained

THINGS THAT WERE FUN OR RELAXING TODAY

....

....

THINGS THAT WERE TOUGH OR STRESSFUL TODAY

....

....

KIND THINGS I DID FOR MYSELF TODAY

....

....

WHAT WAS MY FAVORITE PART OF TODAY?

....

....

HOW CAN I MAKE TOMORROW BETTER?

....

....

NOTES AND REFLECTIONS

Write it down

I RELEASE ALL NEGATIVITY AND FOCUS ON MY OWN UNIQUENESS & DESTINY.

1. _____

2. _____

3. _____

4. _____

5. _____

6. _____

7. _____

8. _____

9. _____

10. _____

When was the last time I tried something new?

....
....
....
....
....
....
....
....
....
....
....
....
....
....
....
....
....
....
....
....
....
....
....

DATE: ____ / ____ / ____   M   T   W   T   F   S   S

TODAY I WANT TO FEEL: ....

AN INTENTION FOR THE DAY: ....

DAILY AFFIRMATION: ....

TO DO

6:00AM ....

7:00AM ....

8:00AM ....

9:00AM ....

10:00AM ....

11:00AM ....

12:00PM ....

1:00PM ....

2:00PM ....

3:00PM ....

4:00PM ....

5:00PM ....

6:00PM ....

7:00PM ....

8:00PM ....

9:00PM ....

10:00PM ....

MOOD

MEAL PLAN

WATER   ⬡ ⬡ ⬡ ⬡ ⬡ ⬡ ⬡ ⬡

BREAKFAST ....

LUNCH ....

DINNER ....

EXERCISE

☐ ....

☐ ....

☐ ....

☐ ....

MAIN GOALS

☐ ....

☐ ....

☐ ....

☐ ....

SELF-CARE	TODAY'S WINS	TODAY I'M GRATEFUL FOR
♡	☐	....
♡	☐	....
♡	☐	....
♡	☐	....

PHYSICALLY, EMOTIONALLY AND MENTALLY I FELT

☐ Relaxed	☐ Joyful	☐ Loved	☐ Vulnerable	☐ Mad
☐ Energized	☐ Grateful	☐ Peaceful	☐ Misunderstood	☐ Sore
☐ Well-rested	☐ Optimistic	☐ Valued	☐ Stressed	☐ Weak
☐ Inspired	☐ Excited	☐ Unmotivated	☐ Irritated	☐ Upset
☐ Motivated	☐ Fulfilled	☐ Nervous	☐ Depressed	☐ Tired
☐ Creative	☐ Hopeful	☐ Frustrated	☐ Anxious	☐ Drained

THINGS THAT WERE FUN OR RELAXING TODAY

....

....

THINGS THAT WERE TOUGH OR STRESSFUL TODAY

....

....

KIND THINGS I DID FOR MYSELF TODAY

....

....

WHAT WAS MY FAVORITE PART OF TODAY?

....

....

HOW CAN I MAKE TOMORROW BETTER?

....

....

NOTES AND REFLECTIONS

"

I have a lot of things to prove to myself.

One is that I can live my life

fearlessly.

Oprah Winfrey

The best bit of advice I could give to a younger me is...

....

....

....

....

....

....

....

....

....

....

....

....

....

....

....

....

....

....

....

....

....

....

....

DATE: ____ / ____ / ____   M   T   W   T   F   S   S

TODAY I WANT TO FEEL: ....

AN INTENTION FOR THE DAY: ....

DAILY AFFIRMATION: ....

TO DO

6:00AM ....

7:00AM ....

8:00AM ....

9:00AM ....

10:00AM ....

11:00AM ....

12:00PM ....

1:00PM ....

2:00PM ....

3:00PM ....

4:00PM ....

5:00PM ....

6:00PM ....

7:00PM ....

8:00PM ....

9:00PM ....

10:00PM ....

MOOD

MEAL PLAN

WATER   ○ ○ ○ ○ ○ ○ ○ ○

BREAKFAST ....

LUNCH ....

DINNER ....

EXERCISE

☐ ....

☐ ....

☐ ....

☐ ....

MAIN GOALS

☐ ....

☐ ....

☐ ....

☐ ....

SELF-CARE	TODAY'S WINS	TODAY I'M GRATEFUL FOR
♡	☐	....
♡	☐	....
♡	☐	....
♡	☐	....

PHYSICALLY, EMOTIONALLY AND MENTALLY I FELT

☐ Relaxed	☐ Joyful	☐ Loved	☐ Vulnerable	☐ Mad
☐ Energized	☐ Grateful	☐ Peaceful	☐ Misunderstood	☐ Sore
☐ Well-rested	☐ Optimistic	☐ Valued	☐ Stressed	☐ Weak
☐ Inspired	☐ Excited	☐ Unmotivated	☐ Irritated	☐ Upset
☐ Motivated	☐ Fulfilled	☐ Nervous	☐ Depressed	☐ Tired
☐ Creative	☐ Hopeful	☐ Frustrated	☐ Anxious	☐ Drained

THINGS THAT WERE FUN OR RELAXING TODAY

....

....

THINGS THAT WERE TOUGH OR STRESSFUL TODAY

....

....

KIND THINGS I DID FOR MYSELF TODAY

....

....

WHAT WAS MY FAVORITE PART OF TODAY?

....

....

HOW CAN I MAKE TOMORROW BETTER?

....

....

NOTES AND REFLECTIONS

Read out loud

I HAVE THE POWER TO CREATE THE LIFE I WANT.

I MOVE IN ALIGNMENT WITH MY HIGHEST SELF.

I AM WORTHY.

What is something I wish someone else would tell me? How can I tell myself that more often?

....
....
....
....
....
....
....
....
....
....
....
....
....
....
....
....
....
....
....
....
....
....

DATE: ___ / ___ / ___   M   T   W   T   F   S   S

TODAY I WANT TO FEEL: ....

AN INTENTION FOR THE DAY: ....

DAILY AFFIRMATION: ....

TO DO

6:00AM ....
7:00AM ....
8:00AM ....
9:00AM ....
10:00AM ....
11:00AM ....
12:00PM ....
1:00PM ....
2:00PM ....
3:00PM ....
4:00PM ....
5:00PM ....
6:00PM ....
7:00PM ....
8:00PM ....
9:00PM ....
10:00PM ....

MOOD

MEAL PLAN

WATER   ⬥ ⬥ ⬥ ⬥ ⬥ ⬥ ⬥ ⬥

BREAKFAST ....

LUNCH   ....

DINNER   ....

EXERCISE

☐ ....
☐ ....
☐ ....
☐ ....

MAIN GOALS

☐ ....
☐ ....
☐ ....
☐ ....

SELF-CARE	TODAY'S WINS	TODAY I'M GRATEFUL FOR
♡	☐	....
♡	☐	....
♡	☐	....
♡	☐	....

PHYSICALLY, EMOTIONALLY AND MENTALLY I FELT

☐ Relaxed	☐ Joyful	☐ Loved	☐ Vulnerable	☐ Mad
☐ Energized	☐ Grateful	☐ Peaceful	☐ Misunderstood	☐ Sore
☐ Well-rested	☐ Optimistic	☐ Valued	☐ Stressed	☐ Weak
☐ Inspired	☐ Excited	☐ Unmotivated	☐ Irritated	☐ Upset
☐ Motivated	☐ Fulfilled	☐ Nervous	☐ Depressed	☐ Tired
☐ Creative	☐ Hopeful	☐ Frustrated	☐ Anxious	☐ Drained

THINGS THAT WERE FUN OR RELAXING TODAY

....

....

THINGS THAT WERE TOUGH OR STRESSFUL TODAY

....

....

KIND THINGS I DID FOR MYSELF TODAY

....

....

WHAT WAS MY FAVORITE PART OF TODAY?

....

....

HOW CAN I MAKE TOMORROW BETTER?

....

....

NOTES AND REFLECTIONS

"

One of the lessons that I grew up with was to

always stay true to

yourself,

and never let what somebody else says distract you from your goals.

Michelle Obama

What activities, habits or people make me feel unhappy? How can I let them go?

....
....
....
....
....
....
....
....
....
....
....
....
....
....
....
....
....
....
....
....
....
....
....
....
....
....

DATE: ____ / ____ / ____   M   T   W   T   F   S   S

TODAY I WANT TO FEEL: ....

AN INTENTION FOR THE DAY: ....

DAILY AFFIRMATION: ....

TO DO

6:00AM ....

7:00AM ....

8:00AM ....

9:00AM ....

10:00AM ....

11:00AM ....

12:00PM ....

1:00PM ....

2:00PM ....

3:00PM ....

4:00PM ....

5:00PM ....

6:00PM ....

7:00PM ....

8:00PM ....

9:00PM ....

10:00PM ....

MOOD

MEAL PLAN

WATER   ⬦ ⬦ ⬦ ⬦ ⬦ ⬦ ⬦ ⬦

BREAKFAST ....

LUNCH ....

DINNER ....

EXERCISE

☐ ....

☐ ....

☐ ....

☐ ....

MAIN GOALS

☐ ....

☐ ....

☐ ....

☐ ....

SELF-CARE	TODAY'S WINS	TODAY I'M GRATEFUL FOR
♡	☐	....
♡	☐	....
♡	☐	....
♡	☐	....

PHYSICALLY, EMOTIONALLY AND MENTALLY I FELT

☐ Relaxed	☐ Joyful	☐ Loved	☐ Vulnerable	☐ Mad
☐ Energized	☐ Grateful	☐ Peaceful	☐ Misunderstood	☐ Sore
☐ Well-rested	☐ Optimistic	☐ Valued	☐ Stressed	☐ Weak
☐ Inspired	☐ Excited	☐ Unmotivated	☐ Irritated	☐ Upset
☐ Motivated	☐ Fulfilled	☐ Nervous	☐ Depressed	☐ Tired
☐ Creative	☐ Hopeful	☐ Frustrated	☐ Anxious	☐ Drained

THINGS THAT WERE FUN OR RELAXING TODAY

....

....

THINGS THAT WERE TOUGH OR STRESSFUL TODAY

....

....

KIND THINGS I DID FOR MYSELF TODAY

....

....

WHAT WAS MY FAVORITE PART OF TODAY?

....

....

HOW CAN I MAKE TOMORROW BETTER?

....

....

NOTES AND REFLECTIONS

Read out loud

I ONLY ATTRACT
HEALTHY, LOVING
RELATIONSHIPS.

I DESERVE LOVE AND
AFFECTION.

I LOVE MYSELF.

Describe the most unforgettable moment in your life.

....
....
....
....
....
....
....
....
....
....
....
....
....
....
....
....
....
....
....
....
....
....
....

DATE: ___ / ___ / ___   M T W T F S S

TODAY I WANT TO FEEL: ....

AN INTENTION FOR THE DAY: ....

DAILY AFFIRMATION: ....

TO DO

6:00AM ....
7:00AM ....
8:00AM ....
9:00AM ....
10:00AM ....
11:00AM ....
12:00PM ....
1:00PM ....
2:00PM ....
3:00PM ....
4:00PM ....
5:00PM ....
6:00PM ....
7:00PM ....
8:00PM ....
9:00PM ....
10:00PM ....

MOOD

MEAL PLAN

WATER ⬡ ⬡ ⬡ ⬡ ⬡ ⬡ ⬡ ⬡

BREAKFAST ....

LUNCH ....

DINNER ....

EXERCISE

☐ ....
☐ ....
☐ ....
☐ ....

MAIN GOALS

☐ ....
☐ ....
☐ ....
☐ ....

SELF-CARE	TODAY'S WINS	TODAY I'M GRATEFUL FOR
♡	☐	....
♡	☐	....
♡	☐	....
♡	☐	....

PHYSICALLY, EMOTIONALLY AND MENTALLY I FELT

☐ Relaxed	☐ Joyful	☐ Loved	☐ Vulnerable	☐ Mad
☐ Energized	☐ Grateful	☐ Peaceful	☐ Misunderstood	☐ Sore
☐ Well-rested	☐ Optimistic	☐ Valued	☐ Stressed	☐ Weak
☐ Inspired	☐ Excited	☐ Unmotivated	☐ Irritated	☐ Upset
☐ Motivated	☐ Fulfilled	☐ Nervous	☐ Depressed	☐ Tired
☐ Creative	☐ Hopeful	☐ Frustrated	☐ Anxious	☐ Drained

THINGS THAT WERE FUN OR RELAXING TODAY

....

....

THINGS THAT WERE TOUGH OR STRESSFUL TODAY

....

....

KIND THINGS I DID FOR MYSELF TODAY

....

....

WHAT WAS MY FAVORITE PART OF TODAY?

....

....

HOW CAN I MAKE TOMORROW BETTER?

....

....

NOTES AND REFLECTIONS

I DESERVE RESPECT AND LOVE REGARDLESS OF THE INEQUALITY IN THIS WORLD.

1.

2.

3.

4.

5.

6.

7.

8.

9.

10.

What could I do to make my life more joyful every day?

....
....
....
....
....
....
....
....
....
....
....
....
....
....
....
....
....
....
....
....
....
....
....

DATE: ___ / ___ / ___   M   T   W   T   F   S   S

TODAY I WANT TO FEEL: ....

AN INTENTION FOR THE DAY: ....

DAILY AFFIRMATION: ....

TO DO

6:00AM ....
7:00AM ....
8:00AM ....
9:00AM ....
10:00AM ....
11:00AM ....
12:00PM ....
1:00PM ....
2:00PM ....
3:00PM ....
4:00PM ....
5:00PM ....
6:00PM ....
7:00PM ....
8:00PM ....
9:00PM ....
10:00PM ....

MOOD

MEAL PLAN

WATER   ◌ ◌ ◌ ◌ ◌ ◌ ◌ ◌

BREAKFAST ....

LUNCH ....

DINNER ....

EXERCISE

☐ ....
☐ ....
☐ ....
☐ ....

MAIN GOALS

☐ ....
☐ ....
☐ ....
☐ ....

SELF-CARE	TODAY'S WINS	TODAY I'M GRATEFUL FOR
♡	☐	....
♡	☐	....
♡	☐	....
♡	☐	....

PHYSICALLY, EMOTIONALLY AND MENTALLY I FELT

☐ Relaxed ☐ Joyful ☐ Loved ☐ Vulnerable ☐ Mad

☐ Energized ☐ Grateful ☐ Peaceful ☐ Misunderstood ☐ Sore

☐ Well-rested ☐ Optimistic ☐ Valued ☐ Stressed ☐ Weak

☐ Inspired ☐ Excited ☐ Unmotivated ☐ Irritated ☐ Upset

☐ Motivated ☐ Fulfilled ☐ Nervous ☐ Depressed ☐ Tired

☐ Creative ☐ Hopeful ☐ Frustrated ☐ Anxious ☐ Drained

THINGS THAT WERE FUN OR RELAXING TODAY

....

....

THINGS THAT WERE TOUGH OR STRESSFUL TODAY

....

....

KIND THINGS I DID FOR MYSELF TODAY

....

....

WHAT WAS MY FAVORITE PART OF TODAY?

....

....

HOW CAN I MAKE TOMORROW BETTER?

....

....

NOTES AND REFLECTIONS

"

Your

self-worth

is determined by you.

You don't have to depend on
someone telling you

who you are.

Beyoncé

What do I struggle to love most about myself? What can I do to begin to love that part of myself?

....
....
....
....
....
....
....
....
....
....
....
....
....
....
....
....
....
....
....
....

DATE: ____ / ____ / ____   M   T   W   T   F   S   S

TODAY I WANT TO FEEL: ....

AN INTENTION FOR THE DAY: ....

DAILY AFFIRMATION: ....

TO DO

6:00AM ....
7:00AM ....
8:00AM ....
9:00AM ....
10:00AM ....
11:00AM ....
12:00PM ....
1:00PM ....
2:00PM ....
3:00PM ....
4:00PM ....
5:00PM ....
6:00PM ....
7:00PM ....
8:00PM ....
9:00PM ....
10:00PM ....

MOOD

MEAL PLAN

WATER   ⬡ ⬡ ⬡ ⬡ ⬡ ⬡ ⬡ ⬡

BREAKFAST ....

LUNCH   ....

DINNER   ....

EXERCISE

☐ ....
☐ ....
☐ ....
☐ ....

MAIN GOALS

☐ ....
☐ ....
☐ ....
☐ ....

SELF-CARE	TODAY'S WINS	TODAY I'M GRATEFUL FOR
♡	☐	....
♡	☐	....
♡	☐	....
♡	☐	....

PHYSICALLY, EMOTIONALLY AND MENTALLY I FELT

☐ Relaxed	☐ Joyful	☐ Loved	☐ Vulnerable	☐ Mad
☐ Energized	☐ Grateful	☐ Peaceful	☐ Misunderstood	☐ Sore
☐ Well-rested	☐ Optimistic	☐ Valued	☐ Stressed	☐ Weak
☐ Inspired	☐ Excited	☐ Unmotivated	☐ Irritated	☐ Upset
☐ Motivated	☐ Fulfilled	☐ Nervous	☐ Depressed	☐ Tired
☐ Creative	☐ Hopeful	☐ Frustrated	☐ Anxious	☐ Drained

THINGS THAT WERE FUN OR RELAXING TODAY

....

....

THINGS THAT WERE TOUGH OR STRESSFUL TODAY

....

....

KIND THINGS I DID FOR MYSELF TODAY

....

....

WHAT WAS MY FAVORITE PART OF TODAY?

....

....

HOW CAN I MAKE TOMORROW BETTER?

....

....

NOTES AND REFLECTIONS

Read out loud

EVERYTHING ALWAYS
WORKS OUT FOR ME.

MY GOALS AND DREAMS
ALWAYS COME TRUE.

I AM BLESSED.

If I could escape to a vacation anywhere in the world, where would it be?

....
....
....
....
....
....
....
....
....
....
....
....
....
....
....
....
....
....
....
....
....
....
....
....
....

DATE: ___ / ___ / ___   M   T   W   T   F   S   S

TODAY I WANT TO FEEL: ....

AN INTENTION FOR THE DAY: ....

DAILY AFFIRMATION: ....

TO DO

6:00AM	....
7:00AM	....
8:00AM	....
9:00AM	....
10:00AM	....
11:00AM	....
12:00PM	....
1:00PM	....
2:00PM	....
3:00PM	....
4:00PM	....
5:00PM	....
6:00PM	....
7:00PM	....
8:00PM	....
9:00PM	....
10:00PM	....

MOOD

MEAL PLAN

WATER   ⬡ ⬡ ⬡ ⬡ ⬡ ⬡ ⬡ ⬡

BREAKFAST ....

LUNCH   ....

DINNER   ....

EXERCISE

☐ ....

☐ ....

☐ ....

☐ ....

MAIN GOALS

☐ ....

☐ ....

☐ ....

☐ ....

SELF-CARE	TODAY'S WINS	TODAY I'M GRATEFUL FOR
♡	☐	....
♡	☐	....
♡	☐	....
♡	☐	....

PHYSICALLY, EMOTIONALLY AND MENTALLY I FELT

☐ Relaxed	☐ Joyful	☐ Loved	☐ Vulnerable	☐ Mad
☐ Energized	☐ Grateful	☐ Peaceful	☐ Misunderstood	☐ Sore
☐ Well-rested	☐ Optimistic	☐ Valued	☐ Stressed	☐ Weak
☐ Inspired	☐ Excited	☐ Unmotivated	☐ Irritated	☐ Upset
☐ Motivated	☐ Fulfilled	☐ Nervous	☐ Depressed	☐ Tired
☐ Creative	☐ Hopeful	☐ Frustrated	☐ Anxious	☐ Drained

THINGS THAT WERE FUN OR RELAXING TODAY

THINGS THAT WERE TOUGH OR STRESSFUL TODAY

KIND THINGS I DID FOR MYSELF TODAY

WHAT WAS MY FAVORITE PART OF TODAY?

HOW CAN I MAKE TOMORROW BETTER?

NOTES AND REFLECTIONS

Write it down

I AM FREE TO CREATE THE LIFE I DESIRE TO LIVE.

1. _____

2. _____

3. _____

4. _____

5. _____

6. _____

7. _____

8. _____

9. _____

10. _____

DAILY REFLECTION

What would I do if I loved myself unconditionally? How would I treat myself? How can I start doing that now?

....
....
....
....
....
....
....
....
....
....
....
....
....
....
....
....
....
....
....

DATE: ___ / ___ / ___   M   T   W   T   F   S   S

TODAY I WANT TO FEEL: ....

AN INTENTION FOR THE DAY: ....

DAILY AFFIRMATION: ....

TO DO

6:00AM ....

7:00AM ....

8:00AM ....

9:00AM ....

10:00AM ....

11:00AM ....

12:00PM ....

1:00PM ....

2:00PM ....

3:00PM ....

4:00PM ....

5:00PM ....

6:00PM ....

7:00PM ....

8:00PM ....

9:00PM ....

10:00PM ....

MOOD

♡ ♡ ♡ ♡ ♡ ♡

MEAL PLAN

WATER   ○ ○ ○ ○ ○ ○ ○ ○

BREAKFAST ....

LUNCH ....

DINNER ....

EXERCISE

☐ ....

☐ ....

☐ ....

☐ ....

MAIN GOALS

☐ ....

☐ ....

☐ ....

☐ ....

SELF-CARE	TODAY'S WINS	TODAY I'M GRATEFUL FOR
♡	☐	....
♡	☐	....
♡	☐	....
♡	☐	....

PHYSICALLY, EMOTIONALLY AND MENTALLY I FELT

☐ Relaxed	☐ Joyful	☐ Loved	☐ Vulnerable	☐ Mad
☐ Energized	☐ Grateful	☐ Peaceful	☐ Misunderstood	☐ Sore
☐ Well-rested	☐ Optimistic	☐ Valued	☐ Stressed	☐ Weak
☐ Inspired	☐ Excited	☐ Unmotivated	☐ Irritated	☐ Upset
☐ Motivated	☐ Fulfilled	☐ Nervous	☐ Depressed	☐ Tired
☐ Creative	☐ Hopeful	☐ Frustrated	☐ Anxious	☐ Drained

THINGS THAT WERE FUN OR RELAXING TODAY

....

....

THINGS THAT WERE TOUGH OR STRESSFUL TODAY

....

....

KIND THINGS I DID FOR MYSELF TODAY

....

....

WHAT WAS MY FAVORITE PART OF TODAY?

....

....

HOW CAN I MAKE TOMORROW BETTER?

....

....

NOTES AND REFLECTIONS

"

Am I good enough?

Yes I am.

Michelle Obama

Is the life that I am living the life I want to be living?

....
....
....
....
....
....
....
....
....
....
....
....
....
....
....
....
....
....
....
....
....
....
....

DATE: ___ / ___ / ___   M   T   W   T   F   S   S

TODAY I WANT TO FEEL: ....

AN INTENTION FOR THE DAY: ....

DAILY AFFIRMATION: ....

TO DO

6:00AM ....

7:00AM ....

8:00AM ....

9:00AM ....

10:00AM ....

11:00AM ....

12:00PM ....

1:00PM ....

2:00PM ....

3:00PM ....

4:00PM ....

5:00PM ....

6:00PM ....

7:00PM ....

8:00PM ....

9:00PM ....

10:00PM ....

MOOD

MEAL PLAN

WATER   ○ ○ ○ ○ ○ ○ ○ ○

BREAKFAST ....

LUNCH   ....

DINNER   ....

EXERCISE

☐ ....

☐ ....

☐ ....

☐ ....

MAIN GOALS

☐ ....

☐ ....

☐ ....

☐ ....

SELF-CARE	TODAY'S WINS	TODAY I'M GRATEFUL FOR
♡	☐	....
♡	☐	....
♡	☐	....
♡	☐	....

PHYSICALLY, EMOTIONALLY AND MENTALLY I FELT

☐ Relaxed	☐ Joyful	☐ Loved	☐ Vulnerable	☐ Mad
☐ Energized	☐ Grateful	☐ Peaceful	☐ Misunderstood	☐ Sore
☐ Well-rested	☐ Optimistic	☐ Valued	☐ Stressed	☐ Weak
☐ Inspired	☐ Excited	☐ Unmotivated	☐ Irritated	☐ Upset
☐ Motivated	☐ Fulfilled	☐ Nervous	☐ Depressed	☐ Tired
☐ Creative	☐ Hopeful	☐ Frustrated	☐ Anxious	☐ Drained

THINGS THAT WERE FUN OR RELAXING TODAY

....

....

THINGS THAT WERE TOUGH OR STRESSFUL TODAY

....

....

KIND THINGS I DID FOR MYSELF TODAY

....

....

WHAT WAS MY FAVORITE PART OF TODAY?

....

....

HOW CAN I MAKE TOMORROW BETTER?

....

....

NOTES AND REFLECTIONS

Read out loud

I LIKE WHO I AM AND WHO
I AM BECOMING.

I COMMIT TO LIVING A
JOYFUL AND HAPPY LIFE.

What are 3 things my past self would love about my current self?

....
....
....
....
....
....
....
....
....
....
....
....
....
....
....
....
....
....
....
....
....
....
....

DATE: ___/___/___   M T W T F S S

TODAY I WANT TO FEEL: ....

AN INTENTION FOR THE DAY: ....

DAILY AFFIRMATION: ....

TO DO

6:00AM ....
7:00AM ....
8:00AM ....
9:00AM ....
10:00AM ....
11:00AM ....
12:00PM ....
1:00PM ....
2:00PM ....
3:00PM ....
4:00PM ....
5:00PM ....
6:00PM ....
7:00PM ....
8:00PM ....
9:00PM ....
10:00PM ....

MOOD

😄 😊 🙂 😐 😞 😭

MEAL PLAN

WATER ⬦ ⬦ ⬦ ⬦ ⬦ ⬦ ⬦ ⬦

BREAKFAST ....

LUNCH ....

DINNER ....

EXERCISE

☐ ....
☐ ....
☐ ....
☐ ....

MAIN GOALS

☐ ....
☐ ....
☐ ....
☐ ....

SELF-CARE	TODAY'S WINS	TODAY I'M GRATEFUL FOR
♡	☐	....
♡	☐	....
♡	☐	....
♡	☐	....

PHYSICALLY, EMOTIONALLY AND MENTALLY I FELT

☐ Relaxed	☐ Joyful	☐ Loved	☐ Vulnerable	☐ Mad
☐ Energized	☐ Grateful	☐ Peaceful	☐ Misunderstood	☐ Sore
☐ Well-rested	☐ Optimistic	☐ Valued	☐ Stressed	☐ Weak
☐ Inspired	☐ Excited	☐ Unmotivated	☐ Irritated	☐ Upset
☐ Motivated	☐ Fulfilled	☐ Nervous	☐ Depressed	☐ Tired
☐ Creative	☐ Hopeful	☐ Frustrated	☐ Anxious	☐ Drained

THINGS THAT WERE FUN OR RELAXING TODAY

....

....

THINGS THAT WERE TOUGH OR STRESSFUL TODAY

....

....

KIND THINGS I DID FOR MYSELF TODAY

....

....

WHAT WAS MY FAVORITE PART OF TODAY?

....

....

HOW CAN I MAKE TOMORROW BETTER?

....

....

NOTES AND REFLECTIONS

Write it down

I AM PERFECT AND COMPLETE JUST THE WAY I AM.

1.

2.

3.

4.

5.

6.

7.

8.

9.

10.

What do I imagine myself doing five years from now?

DATE: ____ / ____ / ____   M   T   W   T   F   S   S

TODAY I WANT TO FEEL: ....

AN INTENTION FOR THE DAY: ....

DAILY AFFIRMATION: ....

TO DO

6:00AM ....
7:00AM ....
8:00AM ....
9:00AM ....
10:00AM ....
11:00AM ....
12:00PM ....
1:00PM ....
2:00PM ....
3:00PM ....
4:00PM ....
5:00PM ....
6:00PM ....
7:00PM ....
8:00PM ....
9:00PM ....
10:00PM ....

MOOD

MEAL PLAN

WATER   ⬡ ⬡ ⬡ ⬡ ⬡ ⬡ ⬡ ⬡

BREAKFAST ....

LUNCH   ....

DINNER   ....

EXERCISE

☐ ....
☐ ....
☐ ....
☐ ....

MAIN GOALS

☐ ....
☐ ....
☐ ....
☐ ....

SELF-CARE	TODAY'S WINS	TODAY I'M GRATEFUL FOR
♡	☐	....
♡	☐	....
♡	☐	....
♡	☐	....

PHYSICALLY, EMOTIONALLY AND MENTALLY I FELT

☐ Relaxed ☐ Joyful ☐ Loved ☐ Vulnerable ☐ Mad

☐ Energized ☐ Grateful ☐ Peaceful ☐ Misunderstood ☐ Sore

☐ Well-rested ☐ Optimistic ☐ Valued ☐ Stressed ☐ Weak

☐ Inspired ☐ Excited ☐ Unmotivated ☐ Irritated ☐ Upset

☐ Motivated ☐ Fulfilled ☐ Nervous ☐ Depressed ☐ Tired

☐ Creative ☐ Hopeful ☐ Frustrated ☐ Anxious ☐ Drained

THINGS THAT WERE FUN OR RELAXING TODAY

....

....

THINGS THAT WERE TOUGH OR STRESSFUL TODAY

....

....

KIND THINGS I DID FOR MYSELF TODAY

....

....

WHAT WAS MY FAVORITE PART OF TODAY?

....

....

HOW CAN I MAKE TOMORROW BETTER?

....

....

NOTES AND REFLECTIONS

"

If I am not

good to myself,

how can I expect anyone else to be,

good to me?

Maya Angelou

What do I judge myself for? What do I
need to forgive myself for?

....
....
....
....
....
....
....
....
....
....
....
....
....
....
....
....
....
....
....
....
....
....
....

DATE: ____ / ____ / ____   M   T   W   T   F   S   S

TODAY I WANT TO FEEL: ....

AN INTENTION FOR THE DAY: ....

DAILY AFFIRMATION: ....

TO DO

6:00AM ....
7:00AM ....
8:00AM ....
9:00AM ....
10:00AM ....
11:00AM ....
12:00PM ....
1:00PM ....
2:00PM ....
3:00PM ....
4:00PM ....
5:00PM ....
6:00PM ....
7:00PM ....
8:00PM ....
9:00PM ....
10:00PM ....

MOOD

MEAL PLAN

WATER

BREAKFAST ....
LUNCH ....
DINNER ....

EXERCISE

☐ ....
☐ ....
☐ ....
☐ ....

MAIN GOALS

☐ ....
☐ ....
☐ ....
☐ ....

SELF-CARE	TODAY'S WINS	TODAY I'M GRATEFUL FOR
♡	☐	....
♡	☐	....
♡	☐	....
♡	☐	....

PHYSICALLY, EMOTIONALLY AND MENTALLY I FELT

☐ Relaxed	☐ Joyful	☐ Loved	☐ Vulnerable	☐ Mad
☐ Energized	☐ Grateful	☐ Peaceful	☐ Misunderstood	☐ Sore
☐ Well-rested	☐ Optimistic	☐ Valued	☐ Stressed	☐ Weak
☐ Inspired	☐ Excited	☐ Unmotivated	☐ Irritated	☐ Upset
☐ Motivated	☐ Fulfilled	☐ Nervous	☐ Depressed	☐ Tired
☐ Creative	☐ Hopeful	☐ Frustrated	☐ Anxious	☐ Drained

THINGS THAT WERE FUN OR RELAXING TODAY

....

....

THINGS THAT WERE TOUGH OR STRESSFUL TODAY

....

....

KIND THINGS I DID FOR MYSELF TODAY

....

....

WHAT WAS MY FAVORITE PART OF TODAY?

....

....

HOW CAN I MAKE TOMORROW BETTER?

....

....

NOTES AND REFLECTIONS

Read out loud

I AM ALIGNED WITH
MY PURPOSE.

EVERYTHING ALWAYS
WORKS OUT FOR ME.

MY GOALS AND DREAMS
ALWAYS COME TRUE.

What personal needs am I sacrificing to meet the needs of others? What boundaries do I need to set for myself?

....
....
....
....
....
....
....
....
....
....
....
....
....
....
....
....
....
....
....
....
....

DATE: ____ / ____ / ____   M   T   W   T   F   S   S

TODAY I WANT TO FEEL: ....

AN INTENTION FOR THE DAY: ....

DAILY AFFIRMATION: ....

TO DO

6:00AM ....

7:00AM ....

8:00AM ....

9:00AM ....

10:00AM ....

11:00AM ....

12:00PM ....

1:00PM ....

2:00PM ....

3:00PM ....

4:00PM ....

5:00PM ....

6:00PM ....

7:00PM ....

8:00PM ....

9:00PM ....

10:00PM ....

MOOD

MEAL PLAN

WATER   ⬡ ⬡ ⬡ ⬡ ⬡ ⬡ ⬡ ⬡

BREAKFAST ....

LUNCH   ....

DINNER   ....

EXERCISE

☐ ....

☐ ....

☐ ....

☐ ....

MAIN GOALS

☐ ....

☐ ....

☐ ....

☐ ....

SELF-CARE	TODAY'S WINS	TODAY I'M GRATEFUL FOR
♡	☐	....
♡	☐	....
♡	☐	....
♡	☐	....

PHYSICALLY, EMOTIONALLY AND MENTALLY I FELT

☐ Relaxed	☐ Joyful	☐ Loved	☐ Vulnerable	☐ Mad
☐ Energized	☐ Grateful	☐ Peaceful	☐ Misunderstood	☐ Sore
☐ Well-rested	☐ Optimistic	☐ Valued	☐ Stressed	☐ Weak
☐ Inspired	☐ Excited	☐ Unmotivated	☐ Irritated	☐ Upset
☐ Motivated	☐ Fulfilled	☐ Nervous	☐ Depressed	☐ Tired
☐ Creative	☐ Hopeful	☐ Frustrated	☐ Anxious	☐ Drained

THINGS THAT WERE FUN OR RELAXING TODAY

....

....

THINGS THAT WERE TOUGH OR STRESSFUL TODAY

....

....

KIND THINGS I DID FOR MYSELF TODAY

....

....

WHAT WAS MY FAVORITE PART OF TODAY?

....

....

HOW CAN I MAKE TOMORROW BETTER?

....

....

NOTES AND REFLECTIONS

Write it down

I FORGIVE MYSELF AND SET MYSELF FREE.

1. _____

2. _____

3. _____

4. _____

5. _____

6. _____

7. _____

8. _____

9. _____

10. _____

DAILY REFLECTION

What can I do today that I was not capable of a year ago?

....
....
....
....
....
....
....
....
....
....
....
....
....
....
....
....
....
....
....
....
....
....

DATE: ___ / ___ / ___   M   T   W   T   F   S   S

TODAY I WANT TO FEEL: ....

AN INTENTION FOR THE DAY: ....

DAILY AFFIRMATION: ....

TO DO

6:00AM ....

7:00AM ....

8:00AM ....

9:00AM ....

10:00AM ....

11:00AM ....

12:00PM ....

1:00PM ....

2:00PM ....

3:00PM ....

4:00PM ....

5:00PM ....

6:00PM ....

7:00PM ....

8:00PM ....

9:00PM ....

10:00PM ....

MOOD

MEAL PLAN

WATER   ○ ○ ○ ○ ○ ○ ○ ○ ○

BREAKFAST ....

LUNCH ....

DINNER ....

EXERCISE

☐ ....

☐ ....

☐ ....

☐ ....

MAIN GOALS

☐ ....

☐ ....

☐ ....

☐ ....

SELF-CARE	TODAY'S WINS	TODAY I'M GRATEFUL FOR
♡	☐	....
♡	☐	....
♡	☐	....
♡	☐	....

PHYSICALLY, EMOTIONALLY AND MENTALLY I FELT

☐ Relaxed	☐ Joyful	☐ Loved	☐ Vulnerable	☐ Mad
☐ Energized	☐ Grateful	☐ Peaceful	☐ Misunderstood	☐ Sore
☐ Well-rested	☐ Optimistic	☐ Valued	☐ Stressed	☐ Weak
☐ Inspired	☐ Excited	☐ Unmotivated	☐ Irritated	☐ Upset
☐ Motivated	☐ Fulfilled	☐ Nervous	☐ Depressed	☐ Tired
☐ Creative	☐ Hopeful	☐ Frustrated	☐ Anxious	☐ Drained

THINGS THAT WERE FUN OR RELAXING TODAY

....

....

THINGS THAT WERE TOUGH OR STRESSFUL TODAY

....

....

KIND THINGS I DID FOR MYSELF TODAY

....

....

WHAT WAS MY FAVORITE PART OF TODAY?

....

....

HOW CAN I MAKE TOMORROW BETTER?

....

....

NOTES AND REFLECTIONS

"

Life is short and it's

up to you to make it

sweet.

Sadie Delany

What would I do differently if I knew nobody would judge me?

....
....
....
....
....
....
....
....
....
....
....
....
....
....
....
....
....
....
....
....
....
....
....

DATE: ____ / ____ / ____   M   T   W   T   F   S   S

TODAY I WANT TO FEEL: ....

AN INTENTION FOR THE DAY: ....

DAILY AFFIRMATION: ....

TO DO

6:00AM ....

7:00AM ....

8:00AM ....

9:00AM ....

10:00AM ....

11:00AM ....

12:00PM ....

1:00PM ....

2:00PM ....

3:00PM ....

4:00PM ....

5:00PM ....

6:00PM ....

7:00PM ....

8:00PM ....

9:00PM ....

10:00PM ....

MOOD

MEAL PLAN

WATER   ⬡ ⬡ ⬡ ⬡ ⬡ ⬡ ⬡ ⬡

BREAKFAST ....

LUNCH ....

DINNER ....

EXERCISE

☐ ....

☐ ....

☐ ....

☐ ....

MAIN GOALS

☐ ....

☐ ....

☐ ....

☐ ....

SELF-CARE	TODAY'S WINS	TODAY I'M GRATEFUL FOR
♡	☐	
♡	☐	
♡	☐	
♡	☐	

PHYSICALLY, EMOTIONALLY AND MENTALLY I FELT

☐ Relaxed	☐ Joyful	☐ Loved	☐ Vulnerable	☐ Mad
☐ Energized	☐ Grateful	☐ Peaceful	☐ Misunderstood	☐ Sore
☐ Well-rested	☐ Optimistic	☐ Valued	☐ Stressed	☐ Weak
☐ Inspired	☐ Excited	☐ Unmotivated	☐ Irritated	☐ Upset
☐ Motivated	☐ Fulfilled	☐ Nervous	☐ Depressed	☐ Tired
☐ Creative	☐ Hopeful	☐ Frustrated	☐ Anxious	☐ Drained

THINGS THAT WERE FUN OR RELAXING TODAY

....

....

THINGS THAT WERE TOUGH OR STRESSFUL TODAY

....

....

KIND THINGS I DID FOR MYSELF TODAY

....

....

WHAT WAS MY FAVORITE PART OF TODAY?

....

....

HOW CAN I MAKE TOMORROW BETTER?

....

....

NOTES AND REFLECTIONS

Read out loud

I LOVE THE WAY I FEEL
WHEN I TAKE GOOD CARE OF
MYSELF.

EVERY DAY I AM GETTING
HAPPIER AND HAPPIER.

What is the difference between living and existing?

....
....
....
....
....
....
....
....
....
....
....
....
....
....
....
....
....
....
....
....
....
....

DATE: ____ / ____ / ____   M   T   W   T   F   S   S

TODAY I WANT TO FEEL: ....

AN INTENTION FOR THE DAY: ....

DAILY AFFIRMATION: ....

TO DO

6:00AM ....

7:00AM ....

8:00AM ....

9:00AM ....

10:00AM ....

11:00AM ....

12:00PM ....

1:00PM ....

2:00PM ....

3:00PM ....

4:00PM ....

5:00PM ....

6:00PM ....

7:00PM ....

8:00PM ....

9:00PM ....

10:00PM ....

MOOD

MEAL PLAN

WATER   ⬦ ⬦ ⬦ ⬦ ⬦ ⬦ ⬦ ⬦

BREAKFAST ....

LUNCH ....

DINNER ....

EXERCISE

☐ ....

☐ ....

☐ ....

☐ ....

MAIN GOALS

☐ ....

☐ ....

☐ ....

☐ ....

SELF-CARE	TODAY'S WINS	TODAY I'M GRATEFUL FOR
♡	☐	....
♡	☐	....
♡	☐	....
♡	☐	....

PHYSICALLY, EMOTIONALLY AND MENTALLY I FELT

☐ Relaxed	☐ Joyful	☐ Loved	☐ Vulnerable	☐ Mad
☐ Energized	☐ Grateful	☐ Peaceful	☐ Misunderstood	☐ Sore
☐ Well-rested	☐ Optimistic	☐ Valued	☐ Stressed	☐ Weak
☐ Inspired	☐ Excited	☐ Unmotivated	☐ Irritated	☐ Upset
☐ Motivated	☐ Fulfilled	☐ Nervous	☐ Depressed	☐ Tired
☐ Creative	☐ Hopeful	☐ Frustrated	☐ Anxious	☐ Drained

THINGS THAT WERE FUN OR RELAXING TODAY

....

....

THINGS THAT WERE TOUGH OR STRESSFUL TODAY

....

....

KIND THINGS I DID FOR MYSELF TODAY

....

....

WHAT WAS MY FAVORITE PART OF TODAY?

....

....

HOW CAN I MAKE TOMORROW BETTER?

....

....

NOTES AND REFLECTIONS

Write it down

I MAKE A DIFFERENCE
IN THE WORLD.

1. _____

2. _____

3. _____

4. _____

5. _____

6. _____

7. _____

8. _____

9. _____

10. _____

What would I regret not fully doing, being or having in my life?

DATE: ____ / ____ / ____   M   T   W   T   F   S   S

TODAY I WANT TO FEEL: ....

AN INTENTION FOR THE DAY: ....

DAILY AFFIRMATION: ....

TO DO

6:00AM ....

7:00AM ....

8:00AM ....

9:00AM ....

10:00AM ....

11:00AM ....

12:00PM ....

1:00PM ....

2:00PM ....

3:00PM ....

4:00PM ....

5:00PM ....

6:00PM ....

7:00PM ....

8:00PM ....

9:00PM ....

10:00PM ....

MOOD

MEAL PLAN

WATER ⬦ ⬦ ⬦ ⬦ ⬦ ⬦ ⬦ ⬦

BREAKFAST ....

LUNCH ....

DINNER ....

EXERCISE

☐ ....

☐ ....

☐ ....

☐ ....

MAIN GOALS

☐ ....

☐ ....

☐ ....

☐ ....

SELF-CARE	TODAY'S WINS	TODAY I'M GRATEFUL FOR
♡	☐	....
♡	☐	....
♡	☐	....
♡	☐	....

PHYSICALLY, EMOTIONALLY AND MENTALLY I FELT

☐ Relaxed   ☐ Joyful   ☐ Loved   ☐ Vulnerable   ☐ Mad

☐ Energized   ☐ Grateful   ☐ Peaceful   ☐ Misunderstood ☐ Sore

☐ Well-rested ☐ Optimistic   ☐ Valued   ☐ Stressed   ☐ Weak

☐ Inspired   ☐ Excited   ☐ Unmotivated ☐ Irritated   ☐ Upset

☐ Motivated   ☐ Fulfilled   ☐ Nervous   ☐ Depressed   ☐ Tired

☐ Creative   ☐ Hopeful   ☐ Frustrated   ☐ Anxious   ☐ Drained

THINGS THAT WERE FUN OR RELAXING TODAY
....
....

THINGS THAT WERE TOUGH OR STRESSFUL TODAY
....
....

KIND THINGS I DID FOR MYSELF TODAY
....
....

WHAT WAS MY FAVORITE PART OF TODAY?
....
....

HOW CAN I MAKE TOMORROW BETTER?
....
....

NOTES AND REFLECTIONS

"

I'm a

Black woman.

Empowered, powerful, and greatness.

Stephanie Lahart

What impact do I want to leave on the world?

Monthly reflections

What went well this month? What did I accomplish? How does it make me feel?

....
....
....
....

What are the most important lessons I learned this month? How did I grow as a person?

....
....
....
....
....

What challenges did I face this month? How did I deal with them?

....
....
....
....

Was there anything holding me back from reaching my goals?

....

....

....

....

....

....

....

What areas of my life did I grow the most in?

....

....

....

....

....

What would I like to keep doing next month that I did this month?

....

....

....

....

....

....

Check out our other manifestation books

Manifestation Journal For Black Women

Do you wish there was an easier way to make the Law of Attraction work for you? Manifest love. Manifest money. Manifest your desires and make your dreams come true with our easy-to-use Manifestation Journal. This workbook is packed with lots of different Law of Attraction techniques, exercises and tools to help you manifest the life of your dreams!

Spiritual Planner For Black Women

Are you ready to manifest the life of your dreams? You can be, do and have anything in 2022! Start taking action and MANIFEST YOUR BEST LIFE NOW!

With the universe by your side, you can climb mountains and manifest a life that is aligned with your heart's desires. With the Law of Attraction, you can have it all and make 2022 everything that you have ever hoped for. Don't wish for a better tomorrow, make it happen! 2022 is the year of the black woman!

Positive Affirmations for Black Women

This book contains a collection of affirmations written specifically for Black women. The words we say to ourselves have immense power and impact over our lives. What you think, you become. Affirmations restructure the dynamic of our brains so that we truly begin to think nothing is impossible.

555 Manifestation Journal for Black Women

We can use the law of attraction to manifest the life of our dreams. We can go from rags to riches, lonely to loved up, and jobless to blessed. There is nothing that stands in our way. 555 manifestation method (also called 5x55) is a fast manifesting technique used for controlling or influencing your energy vibrations.

369 Manifestation Journal for Black Women

You are the creator of your own reality. You are the author of your story. One of the most powerful manifestation techniques is the 369 manifestation method. 369 manifestation technique is a powerful tool to help you attain the life you dream of living. It is perfect for you if you are someone who thrives on following routines when manifesting. The 369 method is where you write your manifestation 3 times in the morning, 6 times in the afternoon, & 9 times at night. This manifestation method is a restructuring system to re-write the subconscious mind. The advantage of this technique is its simplicity and easiness of integrating it into your daily lives.

YOU HAVE ALL THE POWER.
CREATE THE LIFE YOU DESERVE.

That's all for now!

We would love to hear from you! Your opinion matters to us! Share with us how this journal is helping you - it will create a positive change and inspire others!

We create our journals and planners with love and great care. Yet mistakes can always happen.

For any issues with your journal, such as faulty binding, printing errors, or something else, please do not hesitate to contact us by sending us a DM on Instagram @limitlessabundance_official or email info@limitlessabundanceofficial.com

If you enjoyed this journal, please don't forget to leave a review on Amazon.

Just a simple review helps us a lot!

We appreciate your love and support,
it means the world to us.

@limitlessabundance_official

Instagram

info@limitlessabundanceofficial.com

@limitlessabundance

Made in the USA
Columbia, SC
25 September 2024

43028372R00159